THE LADIES OF BEVER HOLLOW, IN TWO VOLUMES: VOL. II

Published @ 2017 Trieste Publishing Pty Ltd

ISBN 9780649623648

The Ladies of Bever Hollow, in Two Volumes: Vol. II by Anne Manning

Except for use in any review, the reproduction or utilisation of this work in whole or in part in any form by any electronic, mechanical or other means, now known or hereafter invented, including xerography, photocopying and recording, or in any information storage or retrieval system, is forbidden without the permission of the publisher, Trieste Publishing Pty Ltd, PO Box 1576 Collingwood, Victoria 3066 Australia.

All rights reserved.

Edited by Trieste Publishing Pty Ltd.
Cover @ 2017

This book is sold subject to the condition that it shall not, by way of trade or otherwise, be lent, re-sold, hired out, or otherwise circulated without the publisher's prior consent in any form or binding or cover other than that in which it is published and without a similar condition including this condition being imposed on the subsequent purchaser.

www.triestepublishing.com

ANNE MANNING

THE LADIES OF BEVER HOLLOW, IN TWO VOLUMES: VOL. II

Trieste

THE

LADIES OF BEVER HOLLOW.

A Tale of English Country Life.

BY THE AUTHOR OF "MARY POWELL."

IN TWO VOLUMES.
VOL. II.

"The bodily frame wasted from day to day;
Meanwhile, relinquishing all other cares,
Her mind she strictly tutored to find peace
And pleasure in endurance. Much she thought,
And much she read . . . and brooded feelingly
Upon her own unworthiness."—WORDSWORTH.
The Churchyard among the Mountains.

LONDON:
Printed for RICHARD BENTLEY, *New Burlington Street.*
1858.

LONDON :
R. CLAY, PRINTER, BREAD STREET HILL.

CONTENTS OF VOL. II.

CHAPTER I.
                                                                        PAGE
Latent Antipathies 1

CHAPTER II.
A Ruse 18

CHAPTER III.
A Family Man 38

CHAPTER IV.
Head and Hands 63

CHAPTER V.
Mr. Glyn in Private Life 74

CHAPTER VI.
Board and Lodging 89

CHAPTER VII.
Mischief 107

CHAPTER VIII.

The same, continued 134

CHAPTER IX.

Merry Christmas 162

CHAPTER X.

Mrs. Althea's Tea-Table 183

CHAPTER XI.

The Sisters Sundered 203

CHAPTER XII.

The Sisters Re-united 231

THE LADIES
OF
BEVER HOLLOW.

CHAPTER I.

Latent Antipathies.

Familiar matter of to-day—
Some natural sorrow, joy, or pain
That has been, and may be again.
                              WORDSWORTH.

"I MUST go—yes, I must go to mamma," thought poor Pamela, on her sleepless pillow, "and tell her all. No, that will never do; she will take me away at once, and I shall lose sixty pounds a year. And yet I feel as if I could not stay... and yet Mrs. Glyn was light-headed; and people are not answerable in that state for what they say. No, but they are for what they habitually think; and Mrs. Glyn must, I fear, have already entertained some such thoughts as those she expressed, or they would not have shaped themselves into words. I do not know how that is—I must ask Mrs. Althea. Yes, it will be better to consult Mrs. Althea than mamma, because she will have all our difficulties at heart: mamma will, for the time, have only mine. Mrs. Althea is dispassionate and yet sympathising—she will tell me whether to go or stay."

And the tired girl turned on her pillow, breathed a prayer, and fell asleep.

George Mildmay rode over to Mrs. Althea the next morning, brimful of things he wanted to say to her, and fervently hoping Mrs. Kitty might be in the poultry-yard, pig-stye, or anywhere but in the parlour.

Wherever Mrs. Kitty might be, Mrs. Althea

to his chagrin, was not alone. Her companion, at first sight, was not ill-looking; her age might be a little above forty; her figure was compact; her features tolerably regular, though sharp; her complexion a little heated; her eyes not large, but black, and as sharp as darning-needles. Her black silk dress and pink neck-tie were unexceptionable, her cap rather juvenile, but very neat; her foot and hand small, but rather stumpy. Such was Mrs. Brand. She was engaged in fabricating one of those works of art which go by the name of antimacassar.

"I'm glad to see you, George," cried she, starting up, and holding out her hand with a very friendly air.

"'George!' who in the world can the woman be?" thought he. "You have the advantage of me, ma'am," said he.

"Well, years have passed since we met," said she, laughing; "I believe it was

'When you were a school-boy aged ten,
And mighty little Greek you knew.'"

"Thank 'e for the compliment, ma'am," says George; "I begin to have an impression of Mrs. Brand. May I make so bold as to ask what has cast you on this bleak, inhospitable shore?"

Mrs. Althea, who had looked very jaded when he entered, was clearing up more and more at every word he said, and was now trying to control a smile.

"I was invited, of course," said Mrs. Brand; "and very sorry have I been, I assure you, to be so long absent from this neighbourhood. I was always partial to it; and I suppose the liking was mutual; for your good people are paying me much attention."

"Beg pardon, ma'am," said George, "but you have not yet allowed me to take my patient by the hand; permit me."

"Certainly; but, dear me, Mr. Mildmay, your

spur is entangled in my knitting-cotton—stay, stop! you'll ruin me!"

George pointed his toe like an opera-dancer, while Mrs. Brand disentangled her cotton; and he finished with a half pirouette, which brought him to Mrs. Althea's side.

"I'm not going to talk over my ailments this morning," said she quietly, as he felt her pulse.

"Just so," said George, in the same key.

"Come, come, you don't escape me in this way," said Mrs. Brand; "I want to hear all and everything, from first to last, and told Kate so this morning when she wanted me to call on those good creatures, the Bohuns. 'Here,' said I to her, 'I shall plant myself, till Mr. Mildmay comes, and till he is gone.' So you've no escape,"—laughing and shaking her ringlets.

"Am I to understand our esteemed friend Mrs. Kitty by the term Kate?" said George. "If so, I take the liberty of remarking it is an abbreviation by which she has never been known in her own family; and as the name of Mrs. Kitty has become endeared among her intimates by long use, and the term Kate has somewhat disrespectful in it—"

" Disrespectful! Why, Kate and I were Kate and Eliza to one another before you were born, Mr. Mildmay, and shall continue so to our dying day, I assure you!"

" Well, I am sorry to hear it," said George, " for Kate always puts me in mind of Petruchio's 'plain Kate, bonny Kate, and Kate the curst.' You remember the passage, I dare say, Mrs. Althea?"

" Oh, Althea's a regular encyclopedia," said Mrs. Brand. " But, do you know, strange as my calling Kate 'Kate,' sounds to you, it strikes me equally odd to hear my two dear friends sunk into Mrs. Althea and Mrs. Kitty."

" *Sunk?* There's been no *sinking* in it, I can tell you!" cried George, fermenting.

"It sounds clownish; in *my* time, they were the two Miss Hills. I see no reason why, simply because they have taken a lower position in society—"

" They *haven't!*" flamed out George.

"Well, well, you know what I mean. Althea understands me. True, they were the Miss Hills of Bever Hollow, and are so no longer; but need it therefore be forgotten?"

"Ma'am, it's not forgotten!" cried George. "There are no two ladies in the whole county more respected, nor so much, as Mrs. Althea and Mrs. Kitty. I go about among all classes, from the highest to the lowest, and know a pretty deal more about it than you do or can, having been out of the neighbourhood, as you say, ever since I was ten years old—"

"I spoke in round numbers; it cannot be so long—nay, I'm persuaded it is not."

"Round, square, or any other numbers, I

speak of what I know, ma'am, and I can swear to what I say."

"Well, well, Mr. Mildmay, you've a rough tongue to your opponents, and a smooth one for your patients," said Mrs. Brand, with a constrained, unpleasant sort of smile. "Though why I should term myself your opponent, I know not, for I am truly glad to hear your testimony to the good report of my dear friends throughout the circle of your practice. It was you who took up the cudgels, no one could say why or wherefore, to fight a man of straw. You remind me amazingly of what you were when I saw you last; and of that illustrative line of one of our poets, 'the child is father of the man.'"

"An odd relation, ma'am."

"A very pretty boy you were at ten, George, I give you my word."

"Oh, ma'am! I had my likeness taken at

that age, so I have some faint idea of what I was—hair rather reddish; face rather full about the cheek and chin."

"Well, your hair *was* a little red."

"Never," muttered Mrs. Althea.

"And when that's the case in boyhood, the whiskers generally betray it afterwards."

"Thank 'e, ma'am."

"Oh, yours are pretty dark, but you can't deceive *me*—I see the golden tinge."

"My dear lady," cried George, "what a blessing it is that I can't retaliate and say I see that your ringlets are sable silvered. On the contrary, you seem to me to have worn remarkably well during the last thirty years."

"Thirteen, if you please!"

"And your appearance is so healthful, that I am certain it must proceed from abundance of exercise in the open air."

"Quite true, certainly."

"Then take a professional man's advice," said he, moderating his tone, "and don't let a little cold weather keep you in-doors. You know, or perhaps you don't know, that you have four hundred and fifty voluntary muscles, which ought to be kept in free exercise, or morbidity will ensue. The air, though cold, is bracing; a long walk, daily, will be of the utmost benefit to you; because, if I were not afraid of alarming you, I should say—"

"What? Pray go on."

"That you have a tendency to fulness in the head—"

"I certainly have."

"Which, if you sit much in a heated room like this, will very possibly induce the morbid tendency I hinted at."

"Are you serious?"

"Perfectly so. Of course, when it hails, snows, and sleets all together, I don't mean you to turn out; but on a fine morning, say like this, with occasional gleams of sun, and the thermometer in the open air not much below thirty, I should say, walk early, and walk long."

"Certainly, certainly. Dear me! four hundred and fifty voluntary muscles—"

"And, as I fancy we shall have a dull afternoon, and Mrs. Kitty has proposed a walk, I would, if I were you, certainly take one."

"Thank you, thank you very kindly. I really will, as soon as you are gone, and we have lunched."

George bit his lip, and rose to depart.

"Mrs. Brand," said he to himself as he rode off, "I dislike you, distrust you, and feel disrespectful towards you. I find pleasure in being rude to you, ma'am. I know you do not like Mrs. Althea, and I am sure she has had reason, some time or other, to dislike you. Why should you come and intrude yourself here, where we were all going on so comfortably together? You'll put your finger into somebody's pie before you are satisfied, I'll answer for it, and I hope it may be burning hot. 'Mighty little Greek,' quotha! You have mighty little manners; and my whiskers are dark chestnut, ma'am, and not carroty; and my loved Mrs. Althea and Mrs. Kitty have not sunk in the estimation of society. They will be 'the *ladies* of Bever Hollow' to their dying day. Mrs. Brand, be very careful of what you do or say, or I will be your open antagonist, and your successful antagonist too."

Meanwhile Mrs. Brand, with uplifted hands, was exclaiming, "My dearest Mrs. Althea, how that fine young man is gone off! Kate's letters represented him in such partial terms, that I really was prepared to find him a finished gentleman, instead of so absolutely bearish and clownish. What man of breeding ever calls a lady *ma'am*, in that pert, offensive kind of way? Besides, there is a degree of frivolity about him which convinces me that he must be quite too superficial for a case like yours.".

"Manner, only manner," said Mrs. Althea. "We are used to it, and call it George's way."

"Way! but what a way. Not the way he should go."

"Well, that is a matter of opinion; but the manner, however boyish and buoyant, which I admit it to be, covers a sound understanding and a feeling heart."

"I must say I think a great deal of manner."

"When George Mildmay enters this room, he seems to fill it with sunshine."

"And that's a great thing," said Mrs. Brand, blandly. "It goes a great way with nervous, anxious patients."

Mrs. Althea was going to reply, but refrained.

"Where can Kitty be?" said she, rather wearily. "I am sure it must be lunch time."

"Shall I go and hasten it?" said Mrs. Brand, officiously. "Do let me just run and steal into the larder, and bring you in the nicest little sandwich in the world; or an egg—we'll boil one in a minute. A rasher? I'll fry you one in five minutes. Do let me be of some service."

"Oh no, thank you," said Mrs Althea, "I was only thinking of you."

"My dear Althea, mine is the most accommodating appetite in the world. I can dine at six with the great, and at—"

"Three with the small, I hope," said Kitty, coming in. "Fie! could not you have said, 'at six with the *late?*'"

"My dear, I should, and meant to have said so. But how sorry I am. Before I came, you dined at one."

"No, we did not."

"At two, then. That unfortunate admission of mine at tea-time, that I was very hungry! You have made this change on my account."

"Honestly, Eliza, I have made it for to-day, and no other, in order that we may have time to walk to the Bohuns'. If we start presently, we shall just avoid interrupting them at their dinner, or having our walk for our pains, which would grieve them."

"That is admirably thought of. I shall enjoy seeing worthy Mrs. Bohun. I suppose she has not a baby always in her arms now. Mr. Bohun, who was such a well-looking man thirteen years ago, is doubtless grown coarse."

"Hardly," said Kitty, doubtfully.

"Not at all," said Mrs. Althea. "Of course he shows the lapse of time; we all do."

"All," echoed Mrs. Brand, "but Kate less than any one I know of. By the bye, Kate, when you came in just now, you put me so in mind of Mrs. Mildmay!"

"Did I?" said Mrs. Kitty, looking flattered. "She was a pretty little woman before she grew so corpulent."

"Please don't use that word, Kitty," said Mrs. Althea.

"Only fit for Mrs. Mildmay's only son," said Mrs. Brand, laughing. "O fie, Kitty!"

"What shall I say then?" said Kitty. "Roundabout? Roly-poly? Come, Eliza, have another egg."

Mrs. Althea, whose aversions in some cases were rather strong, particularly disliked the *gusto* with which Mrs. Brand ate an egg; and was therefore secretly sorry when, after more pressing than an egg was worth, she accepted it. But it was stale! a horrible egg! Mrs. Kitty was quite dismayed, and could not think how it could be. for the date was on the shell;

however, Mrs. Brand would not have another; and so, after a little more chattering and feet-warming over the fire, the two ladies started on their walk, and left Mrs. Althea to silence and repose.

CHAPTER II.

A Ruse.

A whisperer divideth friends.
BOOK OF JOB.

SHE was just becoming deeply interested in a book she was reading—Mrs. Schimmelpenninck's "Port Royalists"—and wishing and praying she might at length attain the heavenly composedness of the Mère Angèlique,—when the door suddenly opened, and George Mildmay re-entered.

"George again?" said she, surprised.

"Have you seen one of my gloves?" said he.

"No," replied Mrs. Althea, looking round.

"Curiously enough, here it is in my pocket," said George. "Well, Mrs. Althea, you and I are now going to have a good coze. I came for that purpose this morning, and was riding homewards, gloomy as night at being defeated, when what should I see but our two fair friends trudging across Collington-common! Thought I, 'There is a tide in the affairs of men!'—and this is mine, so I'll take it. The consequence is, I am here."

"And the glove—" said Mrs. Althea, mischievously.

"Ah, never mind that—there was no sin in a ruse so perfectly transparent."

"Well, but, George, what is the interesting matter—for I am sure it must be interesting—which brought you back? Tell me, my dear friend."

"Ah, that word goes to my heart. Friends we are, and friends we will be. However,—to begin abruptly,—Do you know Mrs. Glyn fell down stairs last night?"

"No! how should I? Poor woman! was she much hurt?"

"Very much, though fortunately she broke no bones. Mr. Forest was sent for in a hurry; he was out; I went in his stead—got there late; was shown up into a wonder of an old bedroom; fitted up in Henry the Eighth's time, I should think. There, on a tall bed all velvet, festoons, and fringings, lay the old lady, held up in the arms of Miss Bohun, who looked as beautiful as an angel. The subdued light of a lamp just caught her hair—"

"Mrs. Glyn's?"

"For shame, Mrs. Althea. Well, you know Miss Bohun is pretty, as well as I do; but somehow, last night there was something higher, more noble, about her mien, than I ever saw before. Her pity was that of a superior being; not anxious and impulsive, as it would have been for her mother; but a kind of dignity accompanied her compassion. Her kind offices were performed in perfect quietness, without anything fussy or officious. Altogether, I was very much struck."

A short silence ensued.

"I have often wondered, George," said Mrs. Althea, "that you have never felt anything like this before."

"I have, but not so strongly. One thing has gone on adding to another, till ... You cannot think how I felt when I first found her living at Bever Hollow! I had gone on, fancying I might speak at any time, and that she was too young, and I too poor, and, in short, that there was no harm or danger in waiting. All at once, the veil was torn away! I had missed my opportunity! To so straitened a family I might have seemed a fair match; to a disengaged heart, I might have been a successful suitor. But now—" He faltered.

"Where is the difference now?" said Mrs. Althea.

"All the difference, my kind friend. She is no longer accessible: perhaps no longer disengaged—"

"I do not believe she is in the way of seeing many to engage her," said Mrs. Althea, drily.

"Many? No, but there's *one*, which is worse. I look on Mr. Glyn as a most dangerous fellow."

"Love's blind, they say; and truly, George, you must be so, if you stumble where there is no obstacle in your path. Mr. Glyn!—I fancy Mr. Glyn would laugh a most insulting laugh at the idea of marrying a nursery governess; for really his little children hardly require more. He is, I am told, one of the proudest of men."

"Well, a proud man may think he ennobles whomsoever he raises to his own position. Besides! the blood of the De Bohuns! . . ."

"A chimera, ten to one, raised for your own torment. I do not suppose he thinks of her at all."

"But perhaps she may think of *him!*"

"You have given her no one else to think about. My dear friend, if you have really well considered this matter, if you really know your heart, do not trifle with your own happiness, and perhaps another's, as so many people do, by delaying to learn how your fate really stands."

"You think I *may*, then?"

"I do."

"My dear, kind friend!"

"I am deeply interested in the welfare of you both. If you are successful, your happiness will make *me* happy too; if otherwise,—why, the sooner you know it the better, and you will meet it like a man."

"Well, the sooner the fates give me an

opportunity—What are you smiling at, Mrs. Althea?"

"I was thinking you were tolerably ingenious in *making* an opportunity of speaking to *me*."

"What, about the glove? Ho! ho! But your governesses are hedged in, like Ecbatana of old, by triple circumvallations. Never mind: 'Where there's a will there's a way.' If I had Mrs. Glyn all to myself, I might keep her tied by the leg these many days; but, you see, Forest will look in and see how things are going, so that won't quite do."

"At the worst, the Christmas holidays will soon be here."

"Aye, the Christmas holidays! She will then go home, of course?"

"I conclude she will. She thought so, I know, before this accident."

"Ha! I must get Mrs. Glyn well as fast as I can, then, I see."

"Pray, George, does my illness depend on your volition as Mrs. Glyn's appears to do?"

"Would that it did!—even if I were not jesting about her. How is it with you to-day? You looked sadly worn when I first saw you this morning."

"Oh, that was only Mrs. Brand."

"Mrs. Brand!—I want to have a good talk with you about her. I was more than ten, as she knows well enough, when she was last here; and my impression is, that she went away leaving anything but an odour of sanctity behind her. What had she been about?"

"George, you have asked one of the most difficult questions in the world. There are some persons of whom you never can complain without seeming captious or fastidious; because the harm they do is brought about by such small and disconnected touches, that it is only their multiplicity which produces the aggregate of evil."

"Just so. We call a person of that sort a disagreeable person, or a mischievous person, just according to the amount and nature of the aggregate. But there must be something to tell about her. Begin at the beginning."

"The beginning was, she and Kitty were schoolfellows, and became cronies. They occasionally spent the holidays with one another, but not often; for my mother, who had a very quick insight into character, did not like Eliza's, even as a little girl."

"Don't call her Eliza. Mrs. Brand is quite good enough for her."

"She was not Mrs. Brand then, she was Eliza Provost; a prettyish girl, daughter of a country attorney in a town twenty miles off. After they left school, she frequently invited Kitty to pay her a long visit: my mother always declined. Kitty at length became hurt, and said her friend was being made to think her proud and unsociable. As a compromise— no, compensation,—my mother allowed Kitty to invite her to Bever Hollow for a month; but she stayed twice that time. In those days, Mr. Bohun and your father, George, were a good deal at our house."

"Looking after *you*, Mrs. Althea!"

"Oh no! It soon became manifest that he was looking after *Kitty*."

"Not at first, though."

"At first?" repeated Mrs. Althea, rather hesitating. "Well, at first, Eliza Provost certainly tried to captivate him."

"That wasn't the first-first, though, ma'am," insisted George. "She tried to get him away from *you*."

"You speak as if you knew all about it already," said Mrs. Althea, faintly smiling.

"I know this much," said George, bending towards her, and speaking very earnestly, "that the other day, in turning out one of the little drawers of my father's old bureau, I found, wedged in at the back, a little yellowish bit of folded paper, docketed in his own hand, 'Althea's hair,' though, on opening it, I found it empty."

"Did you?" said Mrs. Althea, with a tear in her eye. "I—I think I should like to see that paper, if you happen to have preserved it, just to be sure it is no fancy of yours, though I assure you, *I* never gave him any hair."

"Oh, he took it, I dare say," said George, roguishly, "or got somebody else to get it for him,—your sister, perhaps?"

"No," said Mrs. Althea, reflectively, "it must have been Eliza Provost. I remember she quite worried us one day for bits of hair;

just about the time she was beginning to try to please Mr. Mildmay."

"Which she never did, I'm clear!" cried George.

"At any rate, she—Oh, why should we rake up these old things?"

"Why? Why, because they are interesting to us both, my dear friend. Truth lies in a well, and we shall get down to it at last. You see we have already turned up an interesting fact about that lock of hair."

"Though why she should have given him a lock of my hair is very unaccountable," said Mrs. Althea.

"Perhaps that first put her upon finding out he was a marrying man," suggested George. "So then, having made out that, and discerned that he was beginning to feel a tenderness towards you, she tried to divert it to herself."

"At any rate, it ended in its being diverted to Kitty."

"No, ma'am, it *ended*, if you please, in being diverted to my mother."

They both laughed.

"It must be confessed," said George, "the dear, good man was a little *volage*. Well, what ensued after her paying her addresses to my father?"

"George, for shame! My mother saw enough of what was going on to dislike it exceedingly. At the end of the second month, she took care that Eliza should go home. Kitty and your father did not get on much; he absented himself from us, and, in the course of a few months, married your mother."

"Whom I lost too early," said George, sighing. "Well, did anything come of Mr. Bohun?"

"Oh, no. Nothing, nothing. He was only a

friend of the family; a most invaluable, delightful, disinterested friend. Well, we went on very comfortably after that, till Peregrine came home; we then saw much company, chiefly on his account. We had so many visitors, coming and going, that my mother thought Eliza only one among many, who could do no harm; and not only allowed Kitty to stay with her, but to bring her back. Eliza was now older and abler; she got on much better. She set herself to please us all; she especially aimed to please Peregrine, and very, very nearly succeeded. As this was most opposite to the wishes of my father and mother, they mutually interfered and put an end to it. But Peregrine left home in wrath; and Eliza was exceedingly angry too, as much so as was compatible with seeming broken-hearted. She left us all at cross-purposes; my father, chafed with my mother for having, *he* said, been plainer with Peregrine than there was need of; my mother vexed with Kitty for having brought Eliza into the family; and Kitty hurt at my sympathising with my mother. However, it all blew over when we heard that Peregrine had engaged himself in another and an unexceptionable quarter; and very soon afterwards, Kitty received cards and cake from the triumphant Mrs. Brand."

" What a blessing!"

" Mr. Brand did not prove much of a blessing, I believe; for he was an elderly man, of very crabbed temper; but Kitty, who did not go near her friend till some time after my mother's death, said she managed him admirably."

" Managed him! I imagine she did! He did not long trouble her. After his death, which occurred in a few years, she found herself with just enough to maintain an appearance of moderate gentility. Then, at Kitty's instance, she paid us another visit, or rather visitation.

Oh, what an infliction it was! Kitty had visited much in a new circle during her absence from us, and she and Mrs. Brand had a host of subjects interesting and entertaining to themselves, which formed the subjects of allusions and inuendoes in which I could take no part. At length there seemed quite a barrier of division raised up between Kitty and me. Oh, George, how sad it was! I could cry over it when I think of it. I have cried over it dozens of times!"

George groaned.

"My poor father was then confined to his easy-chair by rheumatic gout. I kept with him as much as I could; read to him, wrote for him, talked to him. All at once, Mrs. Brand became very attentive to him. If I left the room for a few minutes, I found her in my chair beside him when I returned. Do you remember her saying this morning, she had *planted* herself here to see you? Well, she used to plant herself beside my father—"

"She sha'n't take root, though, here!" cried George, firing up.

"O George! I hope not! Hark! the clock strikes three,—she will soon return. We had better not speak of her any more."

"I must be off, or she'll catch me!"

"Never *let* yourself be caught! Never let her catch you!—George! see!—She caught, or tried to catch your father, Mr. Bohun, her own husband, my brother, my father, my sister; and if her evil influence should at length extend to *you*—where am I? what will become of me? whom have I left?"

Mrs. Althea cried bitterly. He caught her hand, and held it.

"If you ever find her establishing herself here—if you ever find her getting between me and Kitty: if you find her going about from house to house, sowing gossip and calumnies—"

"Never fear! I'll be even with her!"

"If she begins to steal on you with hints that her dear Althea is very imaginative, very fanciful, very over-wrought, hardly fit to be trusted to her own judgment—her words, her letters to be taken with a grain of salt—"

She was weeping helplessly.

"Mrs. Althea! look at me!"

She looked up at him through her tears.

"Forewarned, forearmed. I knew her by intuition. You have possessed me of facts. Now cast away all fear. I shall watch over you. I shall keep my eye upon her. She shall not do you one grain of harm. Domestically, she may and will be a plague, as long as her visit lasts (by the way, how could you invite her? —oh, to please Kitty, to be sure); but out of doors she shall do you no mischief; nor indoors either, if I can help it."

He stooped his head, and kissed her hand.

"I am your knight," said he affectionately, "as truly as St. George was Una's; and this is my kiss of allegiance. And now good bye, or they'll certainly be in upon us. Professionally, I ought not to have let you talk so much; but you have eased your mind and set mine to work; so now keep as quiet as you can till they return; and afterwards too. Think of something quite different! Think of Pamela and me."

"I will," said she, smiling, and drying her eyes. "I cannot have anything pleasanter to think about."

He pressed her hand once more, and was off. She thought of him and Pamela for several minutes; and then mentally repeated some lines that she had long experienced to be unutterably tranquillizing.

Commit thou all thy ways
To His unerring hands,
To His sure truth and tender care,
Who earth and heaven commands.

No profit canst thou gain
By self-consuming care :
To Him commend thy cause ; His ear
Attends the softest prayer.

Give to the winds thy fears !
Hope ! and be undismayed !
He hears thy sighs, He counts thy tears,
He will lift up thy head.

Through waves and clouds and storms,
He'll safely guide thy way ;—
Trust but to Him : so shall thy night
Soon end in cloudless day.

CHAPTER III.

A Family Man.

Ofttimes it haps that sorrows of the mind
Find remedy unsought, which seeking could not find.
SPENSER.

PAMELA and her young charges had walked rather too late in the damp, leafless shrubbery; and the consequence was, that on the morning after the accident, she found she had caught a severe cold; and the nurse came to her while she was dressing, to say that the children were so poorly, that she had kept them in bed.

Thus, a walk to the Hill House was quite out of the question, even had there been no other obstacles: and things appear so different in the still hours of darkness, and in the bright morning light, that Pamela's alarms had almost faded away: and she found quite enough to think about in the indisposition of her pupils and herself, and in considering whether she had any imprudence to be answerable for. She feared she had been rather thoughtless.

On her way to the children, she passed Mrs. Glyn's door, just as the maid was opening it; and paused to inquire how she had passed the night.

"My dear, come in," said Mrs. Glyn, hearing her voice. "Why, how wan and heavy-eyed you look! You have not been sitting up, I hope?"

"Oh no, dear madam, I have only taken a little cold. How are you this morning?"

"In a good deal of pain. I hope Mr. Forest himself will come this morning, instead of sending that young man. How are the children?"

"I am sorry to say, ma'am, they seem to

have taken cold. Nurse has kept them in bed, and I was just going to see them."

"Pray do so, my dear, and come back and let me know how they are. Nurse did quite right."

On Pamela's return to Mrs. Glyn's room, the door was ajar, and she found Mr. Glyn standing by his mother's bedside. He was saying, "My dear mother, there can be no reason in the world for sending for Mrs. Jay."

Pamela did not wish to hear any more, and thought she might as well go down and make the breakfast. This was a meal the whole family were accustomed to take together; and she had just made the tea as usual, when Mr. Glyn came in, and, taking his accustomed seat, began to open his letters.

"This is an awkward accident of my mother's, Miss Bohun," said he; "but I fancy no great mischief is likely to accrue from it."

"I hope not," said Pamela.

"I shall hear what Forest says about it, however," said Mr. Glyn. "The little girls, too, I understand, are poorly. Colds, I suppose?"

"Yes, sir; and Mrs. Glyn desired to hear my report of them as soon as I had seen them; therefore I had, perhaps, better go to her now; the tea is not quite ready."

"Pray do not hurry back on my account," said Mr. Glyn; "I have plenty to do, you see. My mother fancies I shall be unable to get on without her, and has been talking of having a Mrs. Jay, which would be a great bore; so pray don't encourage it, or let her think I cannot get on perfectly well by myself. In fact, I promised last night to spend the week with Colonel Enderby; and if Forest gives a good report, there's no reason why I should not go. You will send for me, you know, if I'm wanted."

"What *nonchalance!*" thought Pamela rather indignantly, as she went up to Mrs. Glyn. "I could not speak or feel so of my mother. The cases are different, of course: but the accident may prove more serious than he seems willing to think; and, at any rate, while in suspense, he might show a little more feeling. Perhaps he has not much, in spite of his pleasant manners."

"My dear," said Mrs. Glyn, when she had heard Pamela's report, "I think the children are much better where they are; and you will be with them too, and have your meals in the day-nursery, which is a nice snug room. It will be much the best for you to keep in the same temperature, on this floor, as much as you can. It occurred to me in the night, that it would be a nice plan to have Mrs. Jay here till I get about again, which would prevent Charles's feeling lonely. But Charles won't hear of it, and says he would run away from her; so we will get on as well as we can."

Pamela was glad to find Mrs. Glyn had settled her mind so readily and reasonably. She returned to the breakfast-room, and found Mrs. Hutchins and nurse waiting in the vestibule with their trays, to carry up the breakfasts of their respective charges.

"Well," said Mr. Glyn, as he helped himself to cold game, "I hope we are not going to have Mrs. Jay?"

"I think not," said Pamela.

"Mrs. Jay is a thoroughly good creature, but an inveterate proser. Not that I've any objection to *her* coming if *I* go," said Mr. Glyn, laughing. "My mother and you are welcome to have her to yourselves; but, if she comes, I'm off. And I would rather have the privilege of staying, if my mother's case proves in the least anxious. There cannot be a man who less minds knocking about by himself now and then, than I do."

Pamela was very glad to hear it.

"You don't look very well," said he presently, observing her for the first time. "Cold?"

"I believe so—it is not very troublesome."

"I should not be surprised if it went through the house. You had better see Forest. He will dose you all round. I hope I shan't be in for it, hey?—Shouldn't wonder if we were in Forest's books, now, all the winter. We were so once before."

Even Miss Roberta could hardly have seen in this any approach to love-making: but it was all that passed beyond the ordinary courtesies of the table.

When Mr. Forest came, he pronounced Pamela and the children to have incipient influenza, and ordered strict quarantine. Of Mrs. Glyn he hesitated to speak with such certainty of a favourable conclusion, as to make Mr. Glyn quite easy in leaving her. He therefore gave up his engagement to the Colonel, and prepared to make himself as comfortable as a study replete with luxury and a pile of new publications could make him.

Mr. Forest had not seen Pamela in her new character till now, and looked at her a little askance. "So! this is what you have got by having other people's children to look after," muttered he, as he felt her pulse. "You like it, I suppose?"

"Oh yes," said Pamela stoutly, "in every respect except that of being separated from papa and mamma. Have you seen them lately?" and she looked wistfully at him.

"Oh yes. Your mother has a cold: but don't frighten yourself. When I say a cold, I don't mean influenza. You are far more likely to have a severe attack than she is: I just looked in to pay a friendly visit, and ask how you were."

"That was very kind of you."

"Not at all," clearing his throat. "You know I must always take interest in you: especially now that you are turned out of the family nest. I suppose," in a lower voice, "you like your surroundings?"

"Not here, in the day-nursery," said Pamela, smiling and looking at the bare walls, "so well as in our pleasant sitting-room downstairs."

"Here I shall keep you, though, for a few days," said he, laughing, and shaking her cordially by the hand. "Yes, yes," he thought to himself as he left the room, "better up here, with the rest of 'em, in these warm carpeted galleries and air-tight vestibules, than down among the draughts, with that handsome, idle fellow lounging over the fire." Pamela had plenty of guardians.

Later in the day, Mr. Hill and Rhoda called at Bever Hollow. They were leaving cards, when Mr. Glyn, who had seen them arrive, and was feeling rather yawnish, took advantage of a little rain that was falling, to go out to them and press them to come in.

The rain soon ceased; but Rhoda, hearing that Pamela was indisposed, asked permission to go up to the day-nursery; where, rather to Mr. Glyn's chagrin, she remained till her uncle sent for her. A bright thought occurred to Mr. Glyn, that he might ride with them; and while his horse was being brought out, Pamela, who had accompanied Rhoda down-stairs, remained chatting with her at one of the windows.

"Have you seen Mrs. Althea lately?" said she.

"No," said Rhoda, "we never ride there; and I should take shame to myself if the roads and commons had not been in such a state as to be unfit for walking. Mr. Forest, however, said that she has been very ill, but is now better."

"When I look round on these books and portfolios of rare engravings," said Pamela, "I sometimes wish they were mine, that I might lend them to her."

"Pray send her what you like, Miss Bohun," cried Mr. Glyn, who overheard her at the other end of the drawing-room.

"Oh, thank you," said Pamela, colouring, and looking pleased.

"That is—all except the Caracci portfolio," said Mr. Glyn, drawing nearer to her, "and the Vandykes—I presume the old lady would not care much for them, and I should not much care to risk them."

Pamela smiled a little, and was silent.

"Old lady!" cried Rhoda. "We do not consider her in that light at all; and Mrs. Althea has the purest taste for works of art; indeed, I have heard Mr. Mildmay say that some of her etchings were as good as Paul Sandby's."

"Indeed? then she may like to see my Paul Sandby collection," said Mr. Glyn. "As I am not very intimate with Mrs. Althea myself, perhaps you will allow me to entrust the negotiation to you; and if you find they will really give her pleasure, she shall have them."

Rhoda gladly undertook the little commission; and as the horses were now brought round, the riders set forth. Pamela waited to see them mount and ride off; and she thought Rhoda looked fluttered and pleased, as Mr. Glyn arranged her reins and put them into her hand. The drawing-room was delightfully warm: oak logs blazed on the fire; the snow-white rug embedded the feet in its fleecy softness; tempting new books, magazines, and reviews were strewn on the table. Pamela looked around, and thought how she should like an hour's practice on that beautiful grand-piano: stood a few minutes before her favourite Cuyp; and then ran off to the day-nursery.

When market-day came round, a farm-servant brought Mrs. Kitty's horse to the door.

"Dear me, there's a saddle-horse!" exclaimed Mrs. Brand, as she came down to breakfast. "A side-saddle, too!"

"Did not Kitty tell you over-night she was going to market this morning?" said Mrs. Althea. "I think you observed that you should have letters to write."

"Dear me! yes," said Mrs. Brand; "but I could not conceive—I did not understand—I never realized till now—in *what way*—"

The last two words were almost inaudible—a

minute or two afterwards, Mrs. Althea, looking up, saw, to her surprise, Mrs. Brand's face covered with her handkerchief.

"Is anything the matter?" said she.

"Oh, never mind—I shall be better presently—don't take any notice," said Mrs. Brand, rubbing her eyes very hard with her handkerchief. Mrs. Althea complied with her request.

The next moment—enter Mrs. Kitty, in riding habiliments, and jovial spirits. Not seeing Mrs. Brand, who was a little behind the curtain, she went straight up to her sister, whom she kissed, and then, spreading out her riding-skirt—

"Only see, Althea!" said she, "what a nasty jag the habit-pin has made in the cloth!"

"I'll draw it together in a minute for you," says Mrs. Althea.

"Oh no, my dear! I haven't time. We are

late already; and as soon as prayers and breakfast are over, I must be off. Only, I don't think I shall use a habit-pin any more; because, where's the good? I've nobody to take it out for me; and if my habit *does* catch the wind a little, what does it signify? I'm no girl, nor yet fine lady; and when I *was* a girl, folks used to say I had a well-turned ankle, hey?" and she laughed merrily.

"And spoke the truth in saying so," said Mrs. Althea, cordially.

"Truly they did," said Mrs. Brand, emerging from her retirement.

"Dear me, are you down, Eliza?" said Mrs. Kitty, ringing the bell loudly; "we have no time to lose. You've a sty coming in your eye."

"Oh, no," said Mrs. Brand, faintly.

"'Tis so, I assure you." Mrs. Brand coughed, and would have dallied with the subject a little, but Hannah answered the bell, and Mrs. Kitty immediately opened the large Bible. Breakfast immediately followed prayers; and Mrs. Kitty, not keeping her seat two minutes together, was continually popping in and out, giving orders with her mouth full, conning memoranda on her slate, and telling Mrs. Althea, more than once, that if John Twiddy should come, he must call again when she was at home, for there had been an error of two and eightpence in their last settlement.

" What spirits you have, Kate!" said Mrs. Brand, admiringly.

" Oh, what should hinder me of them, on a fine morning like this?" said Mrs. Kitty. " Market-day always puts me in spirits. I expect to do a good stroke of business this morning in the bean-market. I only wish you could go with me."

" *I?*—my dear Kate!"

" Well, I know it can't be, because we

haven't another saddle-horse; and perhaps, even if I had got Farmer Stone to lend us his light chaise, you might not have liked to go in it."

"No, I certainly should not," said Mrs. Brand with constraint, " nor have liked *you* to drive it. The horse is preferable to that."

"For one, but not for two. That's the only thing."

"My dear Kate, what should I do in the bean-market?"

"Oh, of course, no good. Only look about you a little."

"I'd much rather *not* look about me, if I were there," said Mrs. Brand, smiling expressively.

"What! for fear of seeing any one you knew? Dear me, Eliza, if you have any sensitivity of that sort, mine has been worn out long ago, I can tell you!"

"Your spirit is subdued to what it works in," said Mrs. Brand, plaintively.

"Quite," said Mrs. Kitty, with a joyous laugh. "So, ma'am, if you like to see me mount, now's your time. Bring out the chair, Hannah!"

"You dear oddity!" cried Mrs. Brand, trying to give her a caress as she hastened by her. "A chair, indeed! I remember when *that* was not the way you used to mount, Kate!"

"Oh, of course," said Mrs. Kitty, tucking her whip under her arm while she pulled on her strong gloves. "Young girls can spring into their saddles as light as a feather, and young men are very happy to help them; but *I'm* neither young, now, nor as light as a feather, and am very thankful to be as active as I am at my time of life—"

"One would think you were quite advanced in years, Kate!" said Mrs. Brand, following her out.

"Not to see me do this," said Mrs. Kitty,

nimbly ascending to her saddle. Hannah settled her habit; and then, merrily waving her hand, she "laughed and rode away."

Mrs. Brand returned to the parlour and sighed profoundly. Both the ladies knitted for some time in silence. At length Mrs. Brand exclaimed—

" 'Tis no use musing on the past. Regrets are dangerous."

" Yes, I think they are sometimes, though one can't always help them," said Mrs. Althea. "However, musing on the past need not be regretful. I often indulge in it."

" Is it possible?" said Mrs. Brand.

" Why not?"

" Oh, you have such a dreary life to look back upon!"

" We have had some great afflictions, certainly; but likewise many blessings: and even afflictions—"

"Prove blessings in disguise," said Mrs. Brand. "Ah yes, just so—but still, when one's position has very much altered, and one's fortune has very much decreased, and one's expectations have been much disappointed, and one's family and early friends have dropped off,— a single woman has much to deject her."

"I admit it," said Mrs. Althea, touched with sudden pity, as she supposed Mrs. Brand referring to her own case; "your position is isolated at present, I grant, but still—"

"Mine?" cried Mrs. Brand, with wide-opened eyes, and looking half-affronted. "I said *single* women. I was thinking of Kitty and you."

"Oh, we are double," said Mrs. Althea, "and that divides our troubles and doubles our pleasures."

"Well, I can't understand it," said Mrs. Brand. "I always had too sensitive a nature,

I believe. In your position I should be wretched."

" But why ? "

" Oh, every energy would seem ' cribbed, cabined, and confined!' I should so hate to be useless; I should fancy myself such an incumbrance to others! I should long so to help them in whatever they were about; to relieve them of this or that care, to be of some importance in my own little world, to—"

" All this—" began Mrs. Althea.

" To take active exercise," continued Mrs. Brand; "to get to church, to go about among the poor, and among my friends—"

" All this, or much of it, I have felt at times," said Mrs. Althea; " but I have sought and found submission, and the privations are more easily borne than you would think when they are once recognised as coming from our heavenly Father."

"Dear me, yes," said Mrs. Brand; "I have heard many invalids say so. It is quite a common thing, I believe, though I have never been put to any such painful experience. *My* health has always been very good; my spirits have always been very equal: indeed, I've been frequently told that the reason I have enjoyed such fine health is, that my spirits are so equal. Nothing impairs health more than uneven spirits—except uneven temper: so much so, that I declare I am getting more and more into the way, when I hear people complaining of the one, of setting it down to the other."

Mrs. Althea knitted in silence.

"Kate, now, has a golden temper," suddenly cried Mrs. Brand.

"She has," said Mrs. Althea.

"And see what health she has!" exclaimed Mrs. Brand.

"Long may she have it," said Mrs. Althea, faltering.

"Truly, for your own sake."

"Oh, for hers."

"For your own sake, if for no other, I was going to say; for where would you be without her?"

"Ah, I want no reminder of that!"

Another pause.

"Yes; it *is* sad," resumed Mrs. Brand, "when two unmarried women, advancing in years, live together, to think that one *must* survive the other!"

Another pause.

"The surviving one," said Mrs. Brand, reflectively, "could not indulge much in musing on the past, I should think, without regrets?"

Silence.

"Well, I shall go and write my letters."

Bever Hollow.

Mrs. Althea's heart felt as heavy as lead. She stretched out her hand to a thick little book within her reach, George Wither's poems, and sighing, opened on this:

> O! were it not that God hath given me
> Some trials of those comfortings which He
> For men in their extremities provides,
> And from the knowledges of others hides,
> What liberty He gives when we do fall
> Within the compass of an outward thrall,
> And what contentments He bestows on them
> Whom others do neglect, or else contemn—
> Yea! had I not believed Him who says
> That God doth knowledge take of all our ways,
> That He observes each rock within our path,
> With every secret sorrow that it hath,
> That He then nearest is when we bemoan
> His absence, and suppose Him farthest gone—
> Had this been hidden from me, I had here,
> For every line I writ, dropped down a tear.
> But I so oft have found, to my content,
> And felt so oft what comforts God hath sent,
> When of all outward helps we are deprived,
> That (would the same by all men were believed!)
> It might be thought true pleasures were possessed
> Of none but men forsaken and distressed!

"True poet! sincere believer! And he who penned this consolation," thought Mrs. Althea, "lay in the close, sordid precincts of the Marshalsea prison; and therein God gave him spirit to sing sweetly as a lark."

CHAPTER IV.

Head and Hands.

Yet did she not lament with loud allew,
As women wont, but with deep sighs and singulfs few.
SPENSER.

"DEAR me, what a crick I have in my back!" cried Mrs. Kitty at tea-time.

"Ah!" said Mrs. Brand, with a very meaning shake of the head—if any one had but known what the meaning was.

"I hope your rheumatism is not coming back, Kitty," said Mrs. Althea. "The fogs were rising when you came in."

"Oh no," said Kitty, "and the crick is quite gone now."

"I have a theory of my own about that crick," said Mrs. Brand.

"What is it?" said Kitty, who was pouring out tea.

"Another time," said Mrs. Brand *sotto voce*.

"Pray let me hear your theory," said Mrs. Althea. "Kitty's health is as valuable to me, I suppose, as to any one living."

"I believe the crick is a sprain," said Mrs. Brand.

"Oh no," said Kitty.

"Well, I hope it mayn't prove so," said Mrs. Brand.

"How should I sprain myself?" cried Kitty.

"Nay, Kitty," interposed Mrs. Althea, "you are so alert that there are plenty of ways in which you *may* have sprained yourself."

"And one is enough," said Mrs. Brand.

"But I have not done anything beyond common," persisted Kitty.

"What!" cried Mrs. Brand, lifting her hands. "Were you not telling me you had carried Althea to the other end of the room?"

"Oh," said Kitty, colouring, "that was a bit of a brag."

"I wish she had not done it, though," said Mrs. Althea, wistfully. "But you never told me, dearest Kitty, that you had sprained yourself by it."

"Nor did I," said Kitty, stoutly. "This little crick, just now, was only just a little passing prick between my shoulders. I wish I had not been so stupid as to name it. I dare say it *was* a little twinge of my old enemy."

This would quite have satisfied Mrs. Althea if she had not perceived, or thought she perceived, an interchange of looks between her companions. From that moment, she became uneasy.

"What delicious bread this is, Kate!—I beg pardon,—Kitty!" said Mrs. Brand.

"Oh, pray call me Kate, if you like," said Mrs. Kitty.

"Althea does not like it," said Mrs. Brand.

Mrs. Althea held her peace.

"Now, *do* you, Althea?" cried Mrs. Brand. "Be candid."

"Candidly, then, I do not," said Mrs. Althea. "I always think there is a little bad taste in calling any one by a name, or an abbreviation, that is not recognised in their own families."

"I'm answered," said Mrs. Brand, smiling, and nodding triumphantly at Kitty.

"Well," cried Kitty, "sooner than accuse you of bad taste, Eliza, I would hear you call me Kate all the days of your life. So do if you like it."

"Thank you! Then I certainly will," said Mrs. Brand. "It calls up such pleasing memories! Pleasing and painful too!" And she heaved a sigh.

"My father and mother always called me Kitty," said Mrs. Kitty, "and therefore I like the name. But Peregrine often called me Kate; so I like that too."

"How thoroughly domestic you are, Kate, even in your memories! You dwell on the recollections of your family with fond tenderness, while those who admired and sought you are utterly forgotten, or thought of with perfect indifference."

"Why not?" said Kitty. "I should have liked to get married well enough at one time,—to have a house of my own and so forth,—but there never was a man likely to ask me, for whom I cared a halfpenny."

"Kate!"

"Not a straw!"

"Kate!"

"Not a pin!"

"Ah well,—it may have been so.—Certainly, this is the very best butter I ever tasted," said Mrs. Brand.

" Ah, you know my weak side," said Kitty.

" Why, what can *you* have to do with it?" said Mrs. Brand. " Oh!—Aye, I remember. Well, Lady Eleanor Butler and Miss Ponsonby had an apparatus in their fancy dairy for making a pat of butter for their breakfast without soiling their hands."

" Ours is not a fancy dairy, though," said Mrs. Kitty; " we make plenty of butter, and cheese too, for the market as well as ourselves; and our butter fetches a penny a pound more than other people's from the badger."

" Badger! who's he?"

" The dealer that buys up the stock direct from the dairy, without ever letting it get into the market. He has given me a penny a pound more, ever since I buried it."

"Buried what?"

"Why, the butter. We pour the cream into a clean cloth, tie it up like a pudding, put another cloth round it to keep off the dirt, dig a hole, bury it, and in the course of a few hours dig it up again. When poured into a bowl, and stirred smoothly round for a few minutes with a rolling-pin, the buttermilk separates rom it, and there's your butter!"

Mrs. Brand laughed heartily at this, and said she had never heard of such a thing in her life. "Where could you pick it up, Kate? Is it the custom of the country?"

"Oh dear, no; Althea found it in one of her books."

"'Practical Economy,'" said Mrs. Althea.

"You two ought to be called Theory and Practice," cried Mrs. Brand.

"Before I was laid up, I hope I was not merely Theory," said Mrs. Althea.

"Surely no," said Mrs. Kitty. "You always used to attend to the butter and honey. And you keep the accounts still."

"Head and Hands, then," said Mrs. Brand.

"My head is not worth what it was," said Mrs. Althea, sighing.

"Ah, we all feel our faculties decay as time wears away," said Mrs. Brand, soothingly.

Here Hannah entered with a brace of pheasants and leash of partridges, together with a note for Mrs. Althea.

"What fine birds!" cried Mrs. Brand.

The note was from Rhoda; and ran thus:—

"Carlton Hall, Wednesday Afternoon.

"DEAR MRS. ALTHEA,

"My uncle begs you to accept the results of his morning's sport; and I take the same opportunity of mentioning that Mr. Glyn, hearing from me how beautifully you used to etch, will be happy to lend you his collection of etchings by Paul Sandby, if it will give you any pleasure to look them through."

"How very kind!" said Mrs. Althea, who was reading her note aloud. She opened her little letter-case, and wrote a line of glad acceptance to Rhoda, while Mrs. Kitty disbursed a shilling for the bearer.

"Rhoda will soon come to see me," said Mrs. Althea. "She saw Pamela to-day, and found she had a bad cold."

"Who are these young people, pray?" said Mrs. Brand; "and who is Mr. Glyn?"

Mrs. Kitty explained.

"Ah, he may be as good-looking and high-born as you please," cried Mrs. Brand; "but I know I never could bear him."

"Why?"

"Can you ask? Because he occupies Bever Hollow. I shall always consider him a usurper."

"A man cannot be said to usurp what he has bought and paid for," said Mrs. Althea. "We were very thankful to find such a liberal purchaser."

"Yes, indeed!" said Kitty, energetically.

"Well, I'm glad you found him such," said Mrs. Brand. "I hav'n't a notion how much such a place as Bever Hollow might fetch."

The servant entering to clear the table, neither of the sisters thought it necessary to enlighten her; and Kitty presently leaving the room, Mrs. Althea challenged Mrs. Brand to a game of chess. Mrs. Brand declared she should like it uncommonly, but doubted whether it would be civil to Kate to play a game which would exclude one of the three. On Mrs. Kitty's return, however, she brought a cribbage-board with her, and challenged her friend to a game, to which she made no objection. Mrs. Althea smiled inwardly, and took up a book.

"The kitchen chimney's a-fire, mum," said Hannah, putting in her head at the door.

"O goodness!" exclaimed Mrs. Brand.

"Don't flurry yourself, Althea!" cried Mrs. Kitty, running off. "Call the men, Hannah —"

"No, no," cried Mrs. Althea, "empty the salt-box on the fire!"

Kitty gave a look of delighted intelligence and darted out, while Mrs. Brand sedulously re-arranged the overturned cribbage-board. Before she had accomplished this, Kitty returned, scorched, but complacent.

"And the fire?" said Mrs. Brand.

"Out!" said Kitty. "The salt produced some chemical change, and extinguished th flames. There's the advantage, you see, of Head and Hands!"

CHAPTER V.

Mr. Glyn in Private Life.

Would you the bloom of youth should last?
'Tis virtue that must bind it fast;
An easy carriage, wholly free
From sour reserves, or levity;
Good-natured mirth, an open heart,
And looks unskilled in any art;
Humility enough to own
The foibles which a friend makes known,
And decent pride enough to know
The worth that virtue can bestow.
                MOORE'S *Fables for the Female Sex.*

MRS. Glyn, when she found her son had ridden out, sent for Pamela to amuse her.

"I thought I heard a strange voice in the gallery just now," said she; "a female voice."

"It was Miss Rhoda Hill's, ma'am," said Pamela. "She felt herself awkward downstairs without you, and therefore made her way up to the nursery."

"I wonder she came in at all," said Mrs. Glyn. "What need was there for more than inquiries and cards?"

"Mr. Glyn went out to them, ma'am, Miss Hill told me, and begged them to come in, because it was raining."

"Oh, if Charles thought it worth while to go out and press them, that altered the case. I dare say he misses me, poor fellow. But these *parvenus* have a knack of being forward. What do you think of this young lady, my dear? Have you seen much of her?"

"We have met two or three times at Mrs. Althea's," said Pamela. "That is all. Only, there is such an absence of constraint and formality at the Hill House that every one is at ease, and people soon learn to understand one another."

"Humph! And your impression of this Miss Rhoda—"

"My impression is, that she is a very nice sort of girl," said Pamela. "Very gentle, sweet-tempered, cheerful, and accomplished. Not very strong-minded, perhaps."

"None the worse, may be, for that," said Mrs. Glyn, sighing.

"Dear madam, do you think so?"

"I don't know that it adds to our happiness or makes us liked," said Mrs. Glyn. "I am generally thought to have a strong mind; but half my life I have been rowing against the stream—fishing in troubled waters."

"Well," said Pamela, "I feel quite sure that I could neither love nor respect a weak-minded person like a strong-minded one."

"It makes them very yielding," said Mrs. Glyn.

"Not always, I think," said Pamela. "They fret, and are peevish, sometimes, and do not know their own mind about the most trifling things; and sometimes yielding is morally wrong."

"Yes, sometimes : not in the little daily affairs of life."

"I'm afraid I am not very yielding," said Pamela.

"Then you would not suit Charles," cried Mrs. Glyn. "He likes a woman to be as soft as pap."

Pamela laughed, and said she was surprised to hear it. She should have thought he would have liked a little more spirit.

"Oh no! Spirit does not suit him at all," said Mrs. Glyn. "He may amuse himself with it, but he'll never marry a woman of spirit."

"Was Mrs. Charles Glyn very yielding, ma'am?"

"My dear, she was so to excess. She was brought up among Dissenters, but immediately acceded to Charles's wish that she should conform to the Church."

"Did not that show a little indifference, ma'am?"

"Not to *him*," said Mrs. Glyn.

"No, certainly."

"And she preferred town to country; but, to please him, scarcely ever went to London."

"That was very amiable."

"Why, yes... I was against the match at first, not on account of herself, but of her family, and was very cool to her for a while; but really it was so impossible to find anything objectionable in a young woman who never made an objection, that I found I could not keep it up—poor little woman."

"I suppose," resumed Mrs. Glyn, after a pause, "that the Miss Halls are to be ranked among your strong-minded women?"

"Yes, certainly so, I think. Mrs. Kitty would not have embarked in her farming otherwise, nor could Mrs. Althea have supported her long illness so well."

"She has every comfort, I suppose?"

"Yes, except bodily ease. Her friends let her want for nothing."

"Humph! we have never been included among them, and yet one would like to contribute something."

"Mr. Glyn is going to do so, ma'am. He has commissioned Miss Rhoda Hill to offer her the loan of his Paul Sandby etchings."

"Ho! And do you suppose she will care to see them?"

"Oh yes. She is, or has been, a good artist."

"Does she suffer much, do you think?"

"At times. But she says she gets used to it."

"I doubt if I could ever get used to pain," said Mrs. Glyn, wincing. "Depend on it, Miss Bohun, if she says so sincerely, she must be a strong-minded woman. People say those things insincerely sometimes."

"I am sure Mrs. Althea is not insincere," said Pamela. "But she makes the best of it; from affection to her sister, from an energetic disposition, and from a cheerful submission to the will of God."

"Miss Rickards is another strong-minded woman," said Mrs. Glyn.

"Oh, I don't call her so," said Pamela, laughing; "strong-tempered, rather."

"Well, I believe what is called strong mind, might sometimes better be called bad temper," said Mrs. Glyn. "A strong will, that is selfishly bent on having its own way. People of this kind succeed; but they are not liked. We prefer those who have more address, more finesse."

"Ah, I hate finesse, ma'am," cried Pamela hardily; "and could never practise address."

"Well, you have something intrepid about

you, I can see; but, my dear, you have lived very little in the world."

"Very little indeed," said Pamela, laughing; "but papa thinks—"

She was interrupted by a violent fit of coughing; and Mrs. Glyn, compassionating her, desisted from making her talk, and let her knit in silence, till summoned to the nursery tea-table.

"You had a pleasant ride, I hope, my dear Charles," said Mrs. Glyn, when her son next looked in on her.

"Pretty well, ma'am, thank you. I fell in with Symes coming back, and we had a good deal of talk about his bay mare."

"That would hardly suffice for a pleasant ride, I should think," said Mrs. Glyn, drily. "You went out with companions, I understood."

"Oh, Mr. and Miss Hill. Yes; and the

old gentleman turns out to be a great chess-player. I've accepted a challenge of his, for really there is not a good player hereabouts, and I am getting rusty. Miss Hill—"

"Miss *Rhoda* Hill."

"No, mamma. *Miss* Hill asked me to lunch there to-morrow, and then Mr. Hill and I are to have a set to."

" Well, but Miss Rhoda Hill was your riding companion ? "

"Rhoda—yes. She is a niceish little girl. Oh, I like her, I assure you. But I suspect that her cousins treat her in a Cinderella sort of a way. I shall see a little more into it to-morrow. It is very wrong of them; and, although her position is at present subordinate to theirs, her connexions are better, for her mother was a Vane."

"Indeed! why, *we* intermarried with the Vanes. Not very recently, though."

"No. So I told her, and laughed, and claimed her for a cousin."

"That she is *not.*"

"No; only it amuses one to get hold of something of this sort to laugh about. It makes a starting-point; gives you something in common, which it is rather difficult to find in that house."

"Difficult, and not very desirable," said Mrs. Glyn. "There's the second dinner-bell. So you are going away without asking me how I am."

"My dear mother, you took the word out of my mouth at first coming in. You know you began at once about the Hills. I am afraid you have had a long, lonely afternoon."

"No; when I felt lonely, I sent for Miss Bohun. Go, my dear Charles, go; your fish will be cold."

And, as he went off, she said to herself, "Yes, yes; I sent for Miss Bohun; whenever

I feel lonely, I can send for Miss Bohun. No thanks to you, though, Master Charles."

When Mr. Glyn returned the next day from lunching with the Hills, he went up to his mother in great excitement. Pamela, who was taking up a dropped row of stitching for Mrs. Glyn, remained to finish it.

"Mamma," said he, sitting down by her in her easy chair, "we had quite an event this morning; a shocking one, I assure you. The two eldest Miss Hills had made more of a toilet than ladies generally do so early in the morning, I think; and were in dresses ridiculously thin for this time of year,—clear, and sticking very much out, you know. One of them, whisking by the fire rather carelessly, was in flames in a moment. Mr. Hill and I were deep in our chess, when a scream made me look round, and there was Charlotte, all on fire, rushing frantically towards the door; when what did that noble girl, Rhoda, do, but seize her, drag her back, and fling her on the rug, which she wrapped round her till she extinguished the flames."

" Ah! " cried Pamela.

"Well done, indeed!" cried Mrs. Glyn. " My dear Charles, were not the poor girls dreadfully hurt? "

" Miss Charlotte was carried off in hysterics, and I heard a great uproar going on in the house—bells ringing, men sent for doctor, and so forth. Also a great cry for cotton wool. But—

> The man recovered of the wound,
> It was the dog that died.

Miss Charlotte proved to be scarcely singed: while Rhoda, who saved her life, had awfully scorched her pretty, pretty hands and arms."

" Poor, poor Rhoda ! " ejaculated Pamela.

" Poor Rhoda ! " repeated Mrs. Glyn.

"Yes; I thought Miss Charlotte might as well have kissed her," said Mr. Glyn.

"My dear Charles, consider her own danger, and fright, and pain. She had not time to think about it."

"Oh yes, mamma; *I've* had time to think about it all the way home; and she might have given a kiss of impulse. But there was no impulse."

"But where was the elder sister? where was Miss Hill?"

"Oh, she came running out of the little drawing-room, and, to do her justice, was frightened enough; but she did nothing but scream. She patted the rug down a little on her sister, when the fire was quite out. Then she went off, with her arm round Charlotte's waist, Rhoda following. I, holding the door open for them, said to Rhoda, 'You are severely burnt, I'm sure.' She looked very white, but said, 'Oh, it's of no consequence; I shall get some cotton wool. I am so glad I saved Charlotte!' And her eyes were full of tears."

"Poor soul!" said Mrs. Glyn.

Pamela sighed deeply, and did not go away.

"So you waited," pursued his mother.

"I waited to hear the doctor's report. Mr. Hill, you know, wanted some one to enable him to bear the suspense; for, till Forest came, mark you, we did not know how much Miss Charlotte was burnt, but supposed her very seriously injured: especially as she made so much noise about it. So Mr. Hill and I played out our game, and I mated him, which was not surprising under the circumstances; I don't say it in disparagement of his play at all; I know he wasn't thinking of what he was about. So Forest came at last, and quite eased the poor old gentleman's mind by telling him Miss Charlotte had sustained no hurt whatsoever beyond the fright, which had given her nerves a shock that made it as well for her to keep her room the rest of the day; but that Miss Rhoda was much more injured. Here the poor old gentleman became affected, and murmured, 'Poor Rhoda! dear Rhoda! she saved my dear child's life.' I said, 'No permanent injury to that pretty hand and arm, I hope, Mr. Forest?' He smiled at me and said, 'No permanent injury, but a good deal of present pain.' 'May I go and see my dear girls?' says Mr. Hill, wiping his eyes. 'By all means, sir,' said Forest; so then, you know, I shook hands and came away. I fancy Rhoda came in for a kiss from her uncle at any rate. Mamma, I hope you keep plenty of cotton wool in the house; the children may catch fire some day. It's an awful thing to see, I assure you, a woman all in flames!"

CHAPTER VI.

Board and Lodging.

Hark! how the rain pours o'er the wide champaign,
And swells the torrents rushing down the hills!
Are living things abroad on such a night?
* * * * * *
Some doctor's horse dashes along the road
To distant patient. From his warm fireside
The good man goes, amid the wintry storm,
To some sick couch, perchance to look on death.

MESSRS. Forest and Mildmay had a busy time of it this winter; I am afraid to say how many horses they knocked up. "But then," as George said, "*we* are knocked up too. I wish sometimes, just as I am warm in bed, that the wire of that horrid night-bell would break. I never could see the joke of painting up 'Knock and ring.' People are safe enough to do both if they want you; it's a liberty they never require to be invited to take; and if they don't want you, where's the good? 'Please don't knock and ring, if you can possibly help it,' would be more to the purpose!"

"Ah, you talk with the recklessness of a man in full practice," said Mrs. Althea. "Time was, when you were glad enough to hear the night-bell."

"Well, then, that time is completely gone by. Now that we are quite by ourselves, dear Mrs. Althea, see! here is the crumpled little yellow bit of paper docketed 'Althea's hair.'"

"It—it looks like his hand," said she, after bending over it closely, as if short-sighted—George thought, to conceal a tear. "Thank you—" returning it to him.

"Nay, it's of no value to me; I shall not keep it. If you do not want it, I will put it in the fire."

"Please, don't!"

And her hand was hastily stretched out to reclaim it.

"He was an old friend," said she; "an old and dear friend. So we will not burn this little vestige of his kind and friendly feeling towards me."

"Something a good deal more than that, ma'am, I'm thinking," said George. "However, we'll change the subject. Is it not a bore that I have never been able to get over to Bever Hollow since I last saw you?"

"What has hindered you?"

"The queer old lady likes Forest best! So does that *nonchalant* fellow, her son. 'Forest,' says he, 'I'll be obliged by your giving my mother's case your own particular, personal attention. Old ladies don't get over these things sometimes.' So, what could Forest do, you know? or what could I? I'm going to ride over there this morning, though, because Forest is called away in a different direction.

Well, and where is my dear friend Mrs. Brand?"

"She and Kitty are gone to look at some lodgings; rather against the grain, I suspect."

"Why, she doesn't want to live here always, I suppose!"

"I think she would be very glad to remain with us till the spring. It would be both cheaper and more cheerful than being in solitary lodgings."

"Let her pay for her board, then!"

"My dear George!"

"Let her pay for her board, ma'am, I say! I'll broach the subject to her in the neatest way in the world! Have a *quid pro quo*, at any rate."

"I don't think it would be an equivalent, even if we could accept it with any delicacy. She would then consider herself at liberty to remain as long as she liked: and it would destroy the happiness of my life."

"Perhaps the proposal would frighten her away."

"More likely, make her very indignant. Oh no, George; I must take what comes. However trying such things may be, they are part of the discipline which we need."

"Well, ma'am, if you think so; though I should have real pleasure in broaching the subject to her—"

"I dare say you would!"

"But, since it must not be, I can only regret it. So, now for Pamela and Bever Hollow. Oh, Mrs. Althea, if *she* should like Forest best!"

Mrs. Althea had pretty good reason to know there was no danger of that.

Considering that Mrs. Brand and Mrs. Kitty certainly were not in the house at the time this dialogue took place, the subject started by Mrs. Kitty on her return had a singular affinity to it.

"Althea!" said she, sitting down close to

her sister, and speaking in a low tone, very eagerly, "while we were out, Eliza made a most generous proposal."

"What was it?" said Mrs. Althea, with a kind of presentiment.

"The lodgings wouldn't do," said Kitty, rapidly; "and there seems so little chance of getting any this quarter, the weather being so unfavourable for moving, and so forth, that Eliza, in the handsomest way, has offered to pay for her board and lodging with us while she remains; saying we are so endeared to her that she cannot bear the thought of going before the spring. So, I hope, Althea, every objection is removed. A guinea and a half—no, a sovereign and a half, a week! Half her income, you know!"

". What I feared!" ejaculated Mrs. Althea.

"What do you mean?" said Kitty.

"Not to accept it, on any account, Kitty.

Thirty shillings a week would be no compensation for our loss of independence."

"Don't talk of shillings, it sounds so commercial," said Mrs. Kitty. "Eliza is one of the very few persons, nay, the only one, I believe, from whom we could accept any terms of the sort: but she feels so completely one of ourselves—"

"I don't feel her one of ourselves!"

"That we can, without humiliation, receive an equivalent from her. At least, I know *I* am not above being beholden to my friend."

"It would be no equivalent, dear Kitty."

"O Althea!—What, not for board and lodging?"

"Not for peace and comfort."

"Why, what difference would it make in the way we are going on already? There is no time fixed for her going, you know."

"More the pity; but as long as she is here

only on sufferance, she is in a less formidable position than if she paid for what she had."

"Well, you use very odd expressions, Althea, sometimes, considering how particular you are at other times. Formidable, and on sufferance, indeed! For my part, I consider it a very desirable offer. We secure a cheerful companion for the winter, and at no expense: nay, I'll answer for making it something into pocket."

"Oh, I care for nothing into pocket," said Mrs. Althea. "Why should we take boarders? We never did, when we were worse off."

"Well, we have not time, just now, to pursue the question, for she will be coming in directly."

"Yes, dear Kitty, and that is one of the disadvantages of her being here; we never can, at our leisure, pursue *any* question. It was so about the extra fire; it was so about the Sunday breakfast hour—"

" Oh, don't let us rake up those old grievances. Take time to think about it, as you said to me when she first wrote to propose coming. Take time to think about it, till bedtime: or even till to-morrow morning, if you will. In the meantime, we will say nothing about it."

And away hurried Mrs. Kitty.

She did not give her sister till the morrow, however, to deliberate; but, having assisted her at night in her painful progress to her bed, sent away Hannah, whose aid was always required on these occasions, and sitting down on the edge of Mrs. Althea's bed, said eagerly—

" Well, have you thought about it? "

" About what? " said Mrs. Althea, reluctantly.

" About Eliza paying us."

" I thought I was to have till to-morrow—"

" Yes, but it seems so thankless to hang back, that if you really know your own mind—"

"I do, Kitty. My mind is not to accept her for a boarder."

"Then there's thirty shillings a week literally flung away!" exclaimed Kitty.

"Well, my dear Kitty, we don't want them: at least, we did not before •Mrs. Brand came, and shall not when she is gone. She raises the bills, I know. I was surprised to find the wine running short."

"You have no right to speak of those things if you will not accept an equivalent. You refuse to clear thirty—"

"Clear? No, dear Kitty, there's your mistake! You are looking on it as clear profit, whereas you will find her have her money for her money's worth, every penny of it. A fire in her bedroom, meat for breakfast—"

"Althea, how *can* you be so shabby!—Good night."

"Kitty!—dear Kitty!"

But Kitty was gone. It was the first time she had left her sister at night without kissing her; and Mrs. Althea's pillow was steeped with tears.

"Even George will be against me," thought she, "for he was for a *quid pro quo*. And yet I feel that I am right, and that it will be misery if I yield. O Lord! undertake for me!"

And again these lines were brought to her—

Commit thou all thy ways;

and the angel who brought them, watched by her till she slept.

The first sight Mrs. Althea had of Mrs. Brand's countenance the next morning showed her that she must henceforth expect war to the knife. Had she temporized and accepted the pay, or been insincere and pretended that no monetary obligations could exist between such dear friends, an unsafe, uncertain peace would have ensued; but doing neither, Mrs. Brand decided that she was an avowed and powerful enemy, and resolved on acting accordingly.

Therefore, directly after breakfast, there was a yawn, followed by a long sigh. "Heigho! I must lace on my storm-boots, Kitty, and go lodging-hunting, though the weather is unpropitious; for I am too much for your sister, who has done wisely in reminding me that I am but a stranger and sojourner here."

"You can't go out!" cried Kitty. "It is going to snow."

"I must be quick, then, dear, and start before it begins. Don't expect me before you see me; though that is a stupid expression, isn't it, Kate? Neither sense nor grammar. But you overlook all my faults, dear; and they are many."

"I don't think so," said Kitty.

"You dear kind Kate," cried Mrs. Brand, going up to her and kissing her, "you really are a friend, Kate! a sterling friend!"

And with a look of defiance at Mrs. Althea over Kitty's shoulder, which Kitty could not see, Mrs. Brand, smiling, left the room; equipped herself, with great *fraças*, in ten minutes, and out of the house in two minutes more. Kitty, who had hurried after her, and talked to her at first in a very raised voice and then in a very low one, saw her off, and remained watching her at the front door, in the cold wind, till out of sight; while Mrs. Althea, pierced by the draught, shivered at the fireside and drew her shawl round her. She saw no living face, except Hannah's, till dinner-time.

Then Kitty came in, in perturbation. "It has began to snow *now*, at any rate, and poor Eliza has not returned! If she does not brave it, she may be kept out till dark. Dear me, if she does not soon make her appearance I shall soon be quite uneasy."

"My dear Kitty, you and I used to think nothing of a little snow like this."

"Don't say such things, Althea; I've no patience! ... Oh, here she comes!"

And Mrs. Althea, for once, was glad of the advent of Mrs. Brand.

Kitty gave her a most voluble welcome, and hurried up with her to hear all there was to hear, in Mrs. Brand's room. When she brought her down to dinner, a traveller from the North Pole could hardly have been treated with more *prestige*. Kitty, returning from the dining-room, was bringing her sister half of a fine apple, when, her foot catching in the carpet, she tripped forward and would have fallen on her face, had not Mrs. Althea, excited to sudden exertion, risen hastily from her couch and caught her in her arms; kissing her before she let her go.

Mrs. Brand, standing in the doorway, burst into a laugh.

"A miracle, a miracle!" cried she. "The bedridden walk! See, the beneficial effects of surprise! Well, Althea, accept *my* sincere congratulations for one; and try to keep it up."

Both of the sisters, for the moment, looked petrified.

"Althea *cannot* keep it up, unluckily," said Mrs. Kitty, shaking up the cushions under her panting sister. "I wish she could." And a tear twinkled in her eyes as she bent down and returned the kiss.

"God bless you, Kitty," murmured Mrs. Althea.

Mrs. Brand saw she must, for the moment, lower her tone.

"I am sure I wish she could, as much as anybody," said she, in a softer key. "Do you feel much shaken, dear Althea?"

"A little," said Mrs. Althea.

"And you, Kate; for it was you that got the greatest shake, after all. My dear soul, you might have hurt yourself very seriously, with your head against the fender."

" Yes, if Althea had not saved me," said Mrs. Kitty seriously.

" And by the bye, Kate, where is the apple that caused this mighty commotion? not the apple of discord, but the apple of concord . . . Ha! here it is, rolled half under the table, and covered with dust. This won't do for Althea now: stay, I'll peel it afresh, and make a most delicate little morsel of it. Why I cried out 'A miracle' just now, was because, by one of those jumbles of dissimilar ideas one has sometimes, I could not help thinking of that archbishop's niece, who threw down her crutches before the 'holy coat' at Treves. Another singular instance occurs to me. Do you remember Olivia Staines? A lovely creature, you know! Well, at the age of eighteen, her voice went completely away: nothing could get her to speak out of a whisper; 'she couldn't.' Well, physicians were in vain: her family became seriously uneasy; every one was talking of poor dear Olivia. Well, she came to stay with us; for my mother, who had a notion there was a little temper in it, fancied she could cure it. She went on two or three days. Still, nothing but whispering. One day, we were talking of Harry Brand. 'A flame of yours, Olivia,' says mamma slyly. 'Mine?' cries Olivia, quite aloud. 'A miracle!' cries mamma, and bursts out laughing. You never saw a creature so confused as Olivia. After that, there could be no more whispering, you know. She protested she was as much surprised as any of us at her voice coming back."

"An agreeable surprise!" said Mrs. Kitty.

"But to what does this story apply?" said Mrs. Althea. "What does it illustrate? To what does it refer?"

"Illustrate! Refer!" repeated Mrs. Brand,

looking rapidly from one sister to the other. "Oh, it does not refer to anything! You know I'm the most inconsequent creature in the world."

"Just move your chair the least bit, Eliza," said Mrs. Kitty, who was threading a large needle with coarse packing-thread, "and I'll cobble up that rent in the carpet till it can be done better, so that at any rate it shall not trip any one up."

Mrs. Brand did as she was requested; and Kitty, dropping on her knees, set vigorously to work, and soon accomplished her task. Rising up with her face much reddened, as soon as it was finished,—"There, mistress," said she cheerfully to Mrs. Althea, "that will prevent me from cutting any more capers, I hope: and you from flying to the rescue."

Mrs. Althea affectionately smiled; and inwardly repeated her ejaculation—

"God bless you, Kitty!"

CHAPTER VII.

Mischief.

Faint friends fallen out most cruel foemen be.
SPENSER.

"MAMMA," said Mr. Glyn—who used this address, half from affection, half from affectation—" do you know, I don't at all like the Miss Hills."

"I *never* have liked them," said Mrs. Glyn.

"No; you took up a strong prejudice against them from the first; rather unreasonably, I think. I resolved I would not be unreasonable, but give them a fair trial: the result has not been in their favour."

" Has anything particular resulted, pray?"

" I rode over there this morning, to inquire after Miss Rhoda; and when I arrived, the poor girl was getting a complete rating. I met George Mildmay riding away from the house; he's a conceited young fellow, I incline to think. He had probably been examining the burnt hands, and perhaps may have expressed, as I have done, his regret at the temporary injury to their beauty—nothing more natural—though a young surgeon had better not deal in such speeches. Anyhow, I suppose he had given umbrage to the two cousins; for, as I went in, rather closely on the servant's heels, I heard Charlotte Hill say in the most galling tone, ' You think too much of his attentions!' And when I went in, I found Rhoda positively in tears!"

"Humph!"

"They all looked confused enough. Rhoda as much as any. In fact, she blushed crimson; and when I asked her how she was, could hardly answer me. She soon made an excuse to leave the room: I should have opened the door for her at any rate, but, of course, with her poor, wounded hands. Turning round, I caught the sisters exchanging looks of irony. *My* attentions, too, gave umbrage, it seemed! And so they shall, if those two girls are going to be jealous, and that young prig is going to be officious."

"Take care, Charles, you don't burn your own fingers."

"Trust me for that, ma'am."

"I think the best way would be for you to go near them as little as possible. They are no pleasure to us. Why not quietly drop them?"

"Drop poor little Rhoda? I should be sorry to do that. Besides, the old gentleman is a worthy old gentleman, as times go. It is only his daughters who are offensive; and if I have, as I rather think I have, the power of teaching them a lesson, I will."

"Oh, well, you must do as you please." And Mrs. Glyn composedly took up her knitting; caring very little, apparently, how much Rhoda's peace of mind might be involved in the course Mr. Glyn was about to pursue.

"Talk of a fellow, and he appears!" said Mr. Glyn. "Here's Mildmay riding up to the house now." And he sauntered off to his warm study and newspapers.

"May I have a word with you, Mr. Glyn?" said George, looking very bright and fresh, as they met in the hall.

"Oh, certainly," said Mr. Glyn; "pray step in here."

"The winter has set in with unusual severity," said George, "and prices are rising, and will rise still higher. Coals thirty-six shillings a ton already. We are getting up a little subscription to enable the very poor to have coals, bread, and rice at a diminished rate, and I thought you might like to put your name down."

"Certainly," said Mr. Glyn. "It's a good thing, I suppose? I don't understand these matters much; nor, perhaps (laughing), do you."

"Well, I hope I understand a little of them," said George. "You see, our practice brings us a good deal behind the scenes; so that we know pretty well who are deserving and who are not; who need help, and what sort of help they need."

"Precisely," said Mr. Glyn.

"Here's the paper," said George, "drawn

up by Mr. Bohun, who, again, is pretty well up to these things. You'll find nothing chimerical or extravagant proposed. People put down just what they will; but there are not many names down yet, because I brought it to you early, thinking you should be one of the first."

"Precisely. 'Mr. Hill, ten pounds.' That's pretty fair, isn't it?"

"Oh, it's munificent; but we don't expect many to give at that rate. He's a good-natured man, you see, and I think I'm a bit of a favourite of his."

"'Miss Hill, five pounds; Miss Charlotte Hill, five pounds.' ... Dear me, this is very handsome! 'Miss Rhoda Hill, ten shillings.'"

"Oh, you must not judge of her by that," cried George, eagerly. "There's as much difference between their five pounds and her ten shillings, as between the offerings of the Pharisees and the widow that had but a mite."

"Ah! That's putting it rather strong, Mr. Mildmay."

"Too strongly, I admit," said George, rather ashamed. "However, it's not only what we give, but what we deny ourselves, that constitutes charity. Now, I happen to know that Miss Rhoda Hill has given up eating potatoes, that the poor may have more."

Mr. Glyn burst into a laugh. George looked annoyed. Mr. Glyn, who observed him closely, saw that he did so.

"What good on earth can she hope to do by it?" said he. "The poor girl probably eats but one potato a day; an Irishman eats half a gallon. What a chimera! How absurd!"

"The principle is not absurd," said George. "The consumption of one person set against that of another. And we know that if every one relieved one, all would be relieved."

"Just so. Oh, the principle, as you say, is charming—charming! She's a charming girl, Mr. Mildmay. It was only the diminutive scale on which she could put her principle into practice, that tickled my fancy."

"If we do all we *can*, no more can be expected of us," said George. "Example is something; and I do not think the two elder Miss Hills can daily help themselves to potatoes while their cousin refrains, without feeling their consciences pricked."

"I doubt very much their consciences being so tender," said Mr. Glyn. "I hope Miss Rhoda does not give up her potato for the sake of pricking them."

"Certainly not," said George. "I understand she expressed very simply her conviction that if all or many of the upper classes, who have such variety in their diet, were to give up the use of this one root, which the poor cannot to their satisfaction exchange for any other, there would be enough, at a moderate price, for those who make them their chief food."

"Very fair."

"And, to evidence that she did not preach what she would not practise, she gave up her one potato."

"I wonder if the cook dresses one less daily, Mr. Mildmay. Ha! ha!"

"Miss Rhoda Hill has no control over that. She has made one convert, however,— her uncle."

"Ha!"

"I think she will very likely make another of Mrs. Althea."

"And another of yourself?"

"That's my affair," said George, smiling. "However, not to be closer about my own concerns than other people's, I'll confess that she has. So, you see, this good little creature has actually saved, or will save, four persons' consumption."

"She is a good little creature," said Mr. Glyn, with some feeling. "If we all did as much in proportion, a good deal would be done."

"A good deal," said George.

"Well, I shall put down my name for ten pounds. I don't see why I should give less than Mr. Hill: and here's my money. Now, I'll step up stairs with you to my mother, and tell her about it, and I dare say she will give something too."

In Mrs. Glyn's room they found Pamela and the children; so George, being able to see all his patients at once, was obliged, with chagrin, to abandon the hope of a *tête-à-tête* that time. However, Mrs. Glyn gave him ten pounds for the charitable fund, so he went away with his pockets full of money as well as a heart full of love.

"O Christmas! Christmas!" inwardly ejaculated he, "never did schoolboy more impatiently desire thee! However, thy advent is not far off."

Here he came in sight of Mrs. Brand, who was walking at the rate of a penny-postman. Had a lane or by-road presented itself, he would not have minded making a circuit to avoid so obnoxious a person; but he scorned to turn about and fly; while to dash forward without recognition would hardly consist with the manners of a gentleman. He just touched his horse with the spur, therefore, and was preparing to pass her with an amiable bow, when she made him a sign to stop, which he instantly obeyed, fearing it might have something to do with Mrs. Althea.

"My dear Mr. Mildmay," began she, in a bland voice, "this opportunity is most fortunate, for I have long been desirous of a short private conference."

"I am always at the service of the ladies, ma'am," said George; "but might not a better time and place be found? This wind cuts like a knife, and you are standing in a puddle."

"I am in goloshes," said Mrs. Brand; "but pray walk your horse gently, and we shall have the wind behind us. Oh, Mr. Mildmay, I'm *very* anxious about my dear friend! . . ."

"About Mrs. Althea?" said George, hastily.

"About Kate," said Mrs. Brand. "Of course, we are all anxious about Althea, but she has now been going on so long, that our sympathies, you know, are getting a little worn out. Whereas, dear, cheerful Kate has such courage and sprightliness that nobody suspects anything is the matter with *her*."

"What is the matter with her, ma'am?" said George. "The last time I called at the Hill House, I heard her whistling in the pantry."

"Ah, that was her way of keeping up Althea's spirits," said Mrs. Brand; "she carries it off so well."

"Carries off what, ma'am?" said George.

"This crick," said Mrs. Brand.

"This *what?*" cried George, reining up his horse suddenly, that he might hear what she said.

"My dear Mr. Mildmay," said Mrs. Brand, laying her hand on his bridle, and lowering her voice, though not a creature was in sight, "did you ever hear of Kate carrying Althea from one end of the room to the other, to look at the stars?"

"Never!" cried George. "Did she though?"

"She did, I promise you."

"Hurra! Mrs. Kitty, I honour you for it!" cried he, with one of his boyish bursts of enthusiasm. "It was famously done of you!"

"Not very famous of Althea to let her do it, though!" said Mrs. Brand with asperity; "I've really no patience with her!"

"Well, it does not look like Mrs. Althea's usual prudence and thoughtfulness for others, I must confess," said George, gravely.

"My dear Mr. Mildmay, you little know a good many things that pass in that house. Why now, what can be more essential to health than a well-ventilated bedroom? And yet Kate, to be within reach of Althea, sleeps in a little closet that has no chimney in it."

"Nay, Mrs. Brand, I know that little room perfectly well, having attended Mrs. Kitty in it more than once; and though, as you say, there is no chimney, there is a ventilator, and the room has always appeared to me perfectly airy—"

"Draughty, if you will, not airy."

"The best proof, ma'am, of it's not being an unwholesome apartment is, that Mrs. Kitty has slept in it these five years and enjoyed robust health. But, about this crick—I want to know—"

"Ah, Mr. Mildmay, *I* want to know, too. But she won't hear of examination or inquiry. She'd kill me, I think, if I hinted it to Althea. My fear is for the spine—"

"Bless me! I must talk a little to my friend Kitty!"

"She won't hear you, I know she won't!"

"But, ma'am, if she won't hear you nor me, what's to be done?"

"Nothing can be done, Mr. Mildmay. With that firm mind, it's my opinion nothing *can* be done. It's deplorable, but cannot be helped. Say nothing, therefore, unless some very favourable opportunity should occur—say nothing at present. Above all, say nothing to Althea!"

"Trust me, ma'am. And now I fear I must wish you good morning. Pray, whither may you be bound?"

"Ah," said she, with a shrug and a smile, "I'm lodging-hunting. I'm one too many where I am—so Althea thinks—and you know what Dante says about the bitterness of another man's bread and the steepness of another man's stairs, when he does not make you welcome to them. So, though I would gladly occupy the little closet without a chimney to be with my dear friends—(and *very* dear they are to me, Mr. Mildmay!) yet, as the feeling is not reciprocated in one quarter, I'm lodging-hunting!"

"But,—in this direction?—What lodgings can you hope to find?"

"Well, I understand Mr. Knight is thinking of moving."

"Indeed? that's news to me," said George, slightly raising his eyebrows. "I thought he must be starving on his practice."

"Don't say I told you—don't spread the report," cried Mrs. Brand.

"Not I, ma'am; *you've* told the person most interested in knowing it!"

"Why, of course, there must be a very poor picking for a medical man in such a small place as Collington," said Mrs. Brand.

"'Tis not the want of population so much as his own want of—well, I'll say no more," cried George. "Good morning."

"*Good* morning!"

And they parted, outwardly, on the most amicable terms.

"I shall go and see about this crick," thought George. "No time like the present.— So Knight is going to vacate the field!— thought he would! An ill-conditioned fellow as ever breathed; didn't deserve to succeed. However, that's between me and myself. What crumbs the bear leaves, the hen may pick up, saith the author of Waverley. I should like amazingly to settle down with Pamela in Collington. We'd soon get roses to trail all over the cottage. Ah, but Mrs. Brand wants it. And, after all, this may be a false report of hers—Knight may not go."

A brisk trot soon brought him to the side approach of the Hill House. Here, looking out of a very small casement, not higher above his head than half the length of his arm, was to be seen Mrs. Kitty, equipped in a dark blue cloth pelisse that had been her mother's, and a round beaver hat. George, after gallantly kissing the tips of his gloves to her, which she returned by smiles and nods, rode over the wet spongy turf, close under her window, and looked up at her just in the attitude of Stothard's Don

Quixote talking to the innkeeper's daughter and Maritornes.

"How are you, Mrs. Kitty?" began he kindly.

"Purely," said Mrs. Kitty; "but Althea has had a bad night, poor love, and is now asleep."

"Then I'll not disturb her," said George. "I shall be this way again in a day or two. Can a fellow say a few words to you without being overheard?"

"Not a creature within earshot," said Mrs. Kitty—"but stay, I'll go to Eliza's window, which is on a lower level than this, for I know she's not within; and there we can talk without raising our voices."

George rode under Mrs. Brand's window, where Mrs. Kitty soon reappeared.

"You are not afraid of the air, in your hat and pelisse, I suppose?" said he.

"Not a bit," said Mrs. Kitty. "Never you fear for me—I'm not going to be upon your books just now, I can tell you."

"Well, I'm not quite so sure about that," said George seriously. "What of this sprain?"

"Then Eliza's been talking to you!" cried Kitty quickly. "She shall catch it!—"

"Sprains are not catching, my dear friend; and seriously, I am anxious about you, and want to know what is the matter."

"Nothing at all is the matter. Eliza took alarm without the least need for it. I'm sure it was very kind of her, but I wish to goodness I had never named the word crick, especially as she came out with it before Althea. It was a little touch of rheumatism, I believe, owing to standing in a draught while talking to John Twiddy; and it has gone quite away—quite away."

"When did you feel it first?"

"About ten days ago. And I did not feel it at all, more than six or seven times. It was just touch and go. There was nothing in it."

"And did you carry Mrs. Althea across the room?"

"Oh my goodness, yes. Where did you get hold of that? Althea told you, I suppose. It did me no harm. She's as light as a feather, and I'm as strong as a horse."

"Still it did not show your sister's usual thoughtfulness to ask you—"

"*She* ask *me?* Surely you know her too well to suspect her of that! No, no; there was no asking in the case. I caught her up, before she could say Jack Robinson. It was only a bit of fun. You know I'm rather frisky sometimes; and I was so just then."

"Ha!—She didn't ask you?"

"No."

"And you feel quite well?"

"Quite."

"Well, I hope you are speaking sincerely; for you well know, my dear Mrs. Kitty, that your life and health are highly valuable to us all, not only on Mrs. Althea's account, but your own."

"George! you're very kind!" And Mrs. Kitty blew her nose very loudly, to disperse some tears that suddenly sprang into her eyes.

"Not at all," said George warmly. "Come, don't get out of sight, I shall think you are using some of Mrs. Brand's rouge-pots."

"Fie, George! that fine colour is all her own."

"Fine colour? High colour, if you will. A very heated complexion. You are ten times better looking than she is, Mrs. Kitty, to my mind."

"George, no soft nonsense."

"You look just like the damsel in Pinelli's

'Serenata,' looking out of that little casement. However, I must not play the cavalier any longer, my dear Mrs. Kitty; so adieu!"

Mrs. Althea was wakened from her nap by the abrupt entrance of Mrs. Brand.

"Well," cried she with a malicious air of triumph, "I've found lodgings at last,—no, a cottage! I may be obliged to let part of it myself, if I find it puzzling to make both ends meet. Rhododendron Cottage!"

"Where on earth is that?" said Mrs. Althea, rubbing her eyes.

"On Collington common. Such a lovely view! Always something to see. On the direct road from one market-town to another. Excellent water, fine air, nice garden, two sitting-rooms, four bedrooms, and offices!"

"It must be a new erection," cried Kitty, who had just entered.

"Ah, I thought I should puzzle you,"

said Mrs. Brand, laughing. "It's Mr. Knight's."

"Mr. Knight's! But, is he going to leave?"

"I never heard his house called Rhododendron Cottage," said Mrs. Althea.

"That's my idea," said Mrs. Brand. "There is a fine rhododendron in the front garden; and one must have an address to give one's friends at a distance. 'Mrs. Brand, Collington,' would not be enough of a direction at first, though it sounds pretty enough. 'Mrs. Brand, Mr. Knight's Cottage,' would be horrid; and quite inaccurate when Mr. Knight no longer rented it."

"True; John Briggs's cottage would be the truer denomination," said Mrs. Althea, "for he built it and owns it."

"Well, whoever built it and owns it," said Mrs. Brand, "it is going to be 'Rhododendron Cottage,' henceforth. I think it sounds well enough, hey, Kate? Better, and less hackneyed than 'Rose Cottage,' or 'Myrtle Cottage?'"

"Much," said Kitty. "I don't remember to have ever heard of a Rhododendron Cottage before."

"But how came you to hear of Mr. Knight's going away?" said Mrs. Althea, with a great increase of cordiality in her tone. "Surely, you did not know it when you went out this morning?"

"I did not; but I called at the baker's on pretence of eating a bun, and he told me there was a report that Mr. Knight was going or likely to go. So, on that, I stepped out. And it *is* a good step. Mr. Knight happened to be at home, so I was able to get at the truth at once. He *is* going: he does not find the Collington practice equal his expectations. Mr. Mildmay undermines him everywhere."

"Undermines!"

"So *he* says. It is his word, not mine. He means to try for better luck elsewhere. He showed me over the cottage. It is small, of course; and the furniture, which is his own, is poor, and somewhat scanty. Altogether, it wants a lady's eye. But, when *my* furniture, which is really handsome, is put into it, and a few cheap alterations made, which can be better done when I am in the house than out of it, it will look quite a different place."

"Undoubtedly it will," said Mrs. Althea, "and the improvements will be a nice amusement for you."

"By the bye, dear Althea, how are you? You were complaining, when I went out."

"Much better, thank you."

"Much better for my having found lodgings, hey?" said Mrs. Brand mischievously. "' Welcome the coming, *speed the parting* guest.' Old proverbs are very rude sometimes."

"I have had a nice nap while you were out," said Mrs. Althea. "It made amends for my bad night. And when is Mr. Knight thinking of leaving? At Christmas, I suppose."

"Well, I am not quite so sure about that," said Mrs. Brand. "We shall see. I must run off now, and change my dress for dinner."

And she left poor Mrs. Althea with a lengthened face, and an inward ejaculation, as she uneasily turned on her sofa. "Ah, she won't go now, it's my opinion. We shall see. Many a slip 'tween cup and lip. Too good news to be true!"

CHAPTER VIII.

The same continued.

Not stayed state, but feeble stay,
Not costly robes, but poor array,
Not passed wealth, but present want,
Not heaped store, but slender scant,
Not wish at will, but weary woe,
Doth truly try the friend from foe.
Paradise of Dainty Devices.

MRS. Brand, returning from her toilette, found Mrs. Althea alone; and sitting down beside her, began with—

"That dear good Kate has been thoughtful for me in my absence. She has nailed a list all round my window to keep out the draught. I cannot but love her for her kindness; though, between ourselves, do you know I think an airy bedroom essential to health."

"Airy, not draughty," said Mrs. Althea.

"Exactly what Mr. Mildmay said—by the bye, I forgot to mention, that I met him on the Collington road. I was talking to him about lodgings. No, that wasn't quite it neither. I forget exactly how it was. But I remember we were talking about the distinction between draughty and airy; and agreeing that an airy bedroom was essential to health. Mr. Knight's bedrooms are very airy. But as I was walking along, it occurred to me to wonder how Kate could keep her health, sleeping as she does in that small closet without a chimney; for you know, Althea, a Canary bird, hung within the curtains of a bed, will die before morning; and it seems to me to account for her having grown pale."

"Pale!" ejaculated Mrs. Althea, "I think Kitty remarkably fresh-looking."

"Oh, my dear Althea! *Was* fresh-looking, I

grant you! But you, who see her so constantly, don't note those changes which strike a stranger."

"You think her pale?" said Mrs. Althea.

"Paler, I don't say pale. Look at her beside me, the next time she comes in."

Mrs. Althea, who knew that Mrs. Kitty's florid face would be pale beside Mrs. Brand's rubicund countenance, said nothing, but yet was disquieted.

"Kate," resumed Mrs. Brand, "has not, I understand, always slept in that room?"

"She slept there some time before my illness," said Mrs. Althea, "thinking it more companionable for us to be together, after a fright we had of thieves one night; the stairs had tried me, and prevented my sleeping upstairs, long before I was regularly invalided."

"That was a pity," said Mrs. Brand, "because I consider the room I occupy the best in the house; and it would have suited you, who like—who *ought* to have the best of everything. And adjoining it is a nice airy room that would have suited Kate very well."

"That room, however, is exactly the size of the one you term a closet," said Mrs. Althea.

"My dear soul, it has a *chimney*. And so great is my interest in dear Kate, that, if she would consent to change rooms with me, which I am sure she would not, I would gladly, for her sake, sleep in the closet."

"You might both sleep up-stairs without any change on your part being needed," said Mrs. Althea.

"What, and leave *you* down-stairs all by yourself?" cried Mrs. Brand. "My dear creature. But here she comes! Mum!"

And with one of her mysteriously intelligent looks to Mrs. Althea, she changed the subject immediately on Mrs. Kitty's entrance. Mrs.

Althea, however, was not to be made a party against her own sister. She had always been accustomed to speak to Kitty with the utmost frankness; and fancying on her entrance, that she really looked paler than usual, she brooded on the subject till a pause in the flow of Mrs. Brand's chat gave her an opportunity of introducing it, and then quietly though anxiously spoke of it to her sister.

Kitty was quite taken by surprise, and disposed to laugh at the idea of the room being close; then provoked at the suggestion, and ready to cry at its being seriously pursued. But Mrs. Brand, though not the ostensible leader, followed it up so warmly and pertinaciously, and Mrs. Althea's nerves were now so tremulous at the idea that Kitty should suffer any injury through her, that it ended in Mrs. Kitty's consenting, with tears in her eyes, to sleep away from Mrs. Althea for a few nights, by way of experiment; on condition that Hannah, for whose health Mrs. Brand seemed to entertain no fears, should occupy the closet.

"What whims! and what changes!" muttered old Hannah to herself, as she tumbled her feather-bed down-stairs. "It's all that Mrs. Brand's doings, *I* knows—Mrs. Firebrand I thinks she ought to be called. And if Mrs. Althea is took ill in the night, I knows whose doing it'll have been, that I does!"

Oh, what a sleepless night it was, to both the sisters! For Mrs. Kitty, in spite of its being her dear Eliza's doing, felt some uneasiness in forsaking Mrs. Althea. Besides, she really was not half so comfortable as in the room to which she had been accustomed; it felt damp, and there was a tremendous draught down the chimney, which kept her feet cold all night.

"I'll have a chimney-board put up tomorrow," thought she. "That's flat!"

In the morning, Mrs. Brand kept up such an unceasing flow of small-talk about her lodgings, her furniture, and her own affairs in general, that she gave the sisters no opportunity of comparing notes on their respective discomforts; and as no considerable harm seemed to have ensued, the sisters magnanimously resolved to be silent martyrs. It cheered Mrs. Althea wonderfully to repeat to herself, "It will not be for long."

"Pray," cried Mrs. Brand, pausing suddenly in the act of helping herself to a second egg, "did it ever occur to you, Althea, to consult Mr. Knight?"

"Dear me, no," said Mrs. Althea.

"Forest and Mildmay have the best practice, all the country round," cried Mrs. Kitty.

"Ah well! how they got it is best known to themselves," said Mrs. Brand, carelessly. "For my own part, if anything were the matter with me, I've a notion I should try Mr. Knight."

"He may be clever, but his looks are certainly against him," said Mrs. Kitty.

"I have never seen him, and never wish to see him," said Mrs. Althea; "but I understand he's not liked."

"I think people are too fastidious," said Mrs. Brand. "To me, his manner was particularly pleasant."

"I am quite content with my present advisers," said Mrs. Althea, with a decision that set the matter at rest.

Immediately after breakfast, Mrs. Brand started off to pay a second visit to Rhododendron Cottage, after vainly endeavouring to persuade Mrs. Kitty to go with her. But Mrs. Kitty had her farming concerns to attend to, and said she must postpone the pleasure. Mrs. Althea was presently left to her own devices;

and commenced with a great fit of yawning, partly from weakness, and partly from want of sleep. Then she read the Psalms and Lessons for the day, and Jay's Morning Portion, and tried to meditate upon them, but found she could not. She was continually recurring to the words, "I wonder if she will go!"

At length she took up her knitting; and before she had knitted many rows, George Mildmay came in. After professional inquiries, "Well," said he, "I was at Bever Hollow yesterday, but to no good. Stay, it was to some good, too; they behaved very handsomely."

And out came his list, with several recent additions to it, which afforded a subject of interest to Mrs. Althea for some time. At length she said, "So you had a little chat with Mrs. Brand yesterday?"

"Yes! what, the woman could not help blabbing, then, though she bound me to secrecy! What did she say?"

"Nothing particular, except that she had found that Mr. Knight was likely to go away, and had thereupon applied for his cottage, and that you had warned her against unventilated bedrooms, and made a distinction between airy rooms and draughty ones."

"That woman! Did she say *I* said that? 'Twas she herself! and with reference to Mrs. Kitty's room."

"Aye?"

"Fact, ma'am. What a twister and perverter of the truth in little things she is! She's dangerous! Every one is, that deviates in small things from the truth; for 'he that despiseth small things shall fall by little and little.' Unfortunately, they make their neighbours fall too. Well, did she get the cottage? She had not seen it when we met."

"I am afraid of being too secure. At first it seemed as though she had taken it; but Mr. Knight is disinclined to give it up at Christmas, and—we don't want her here. But, George, you were afraid she had let out some secret. Come, what was it?"

"The secret was of her own making, though I willingly consented to keep it, because there was no good in worrying you about nothing. She fancied Mrs. Kitty was not quite well—"

"*Is* she quite well, George? Don't deceive me, I entreat you!"

"Right as possible, ma'am. Here she is to speak for herself. Hallo, Mrs. Kitty, your eyes are inflamed. You have caught cold, chatting to young fellows out of open windows."

"Oh no, 'twasn't that," said Mrs. Kitty, "last night was so very cold."

"And she changed her bedroom," said Mrs.

Althea anxiously, " without having a fire lighted in it first."

"That's Mrs. Brand's doing, I know; you need not tell me," said George, looking full at Mrs. Kitty, who felt a little embarrassed.

" Well, she meant it all for the best," said Mrs. Kitty, " and the worst is over now. I've put up a chimney-board."

" Much good the chimney will do you, then," said he, smiling.

Mrs. Kitty, having only come in for the keys, speedily returned to her own affairs.

Almost immediately afterwards Rhoda came in, much to the pleasure of Mrs. Althea, who had not seen her for some time. The cold air had given her a bright colour, but it was considerably heightened on her seeing George Mildmay; and she seemed so embarrassed by his presence, that he saw it, and, smiling, soon took his leave.

"A long time has passed since I saw you last," said Mrs. Althea.

"Oh, too long, a great deal," said Rhoda, eagerly; "and I have so much to say, I hardly know where to begin."

"In the first place," said Mrs. Althea, willing to give her time to compose herself, "I have to thank you for procuring me the loan of Paul Sandby's etchings."

"Oh, did you like them? I felt sure you would. It was Mr. Glyn you should thank, not me. He is so very kind—"

"Is he? I have seen so little of him, that I am glad to hear it from one who knows him better than I do." Rhoda's cheeks again burned. "How sorry I was," pursued Mrs. Althea, "to hear of your sad accident. Do tell me all about it; I have only had George Mildmay's account."

"Oh, my hands are quite well now. See,

they are very little scarred. Mr. Glyn has made more of it than there was any occasion for, and called every day almost, every day but two, to inquire about them; and, you see, dear Mrs. Althea, that, not knowing the ways of the house, he could not guess that this would be ill taken, and in fact, quite mistaken, quite a wrong construction put upon it; and that what he meant for kindness and politeness, and all that, and intended should give me pleasure, only gave me pain; or, at any rate, got me into so much trouble, as very much to damp the pleasure."

"How was that?"

"I hardly know how to tell you, and yet I came here this morning for nothing else. I thought you would tell me what to do. Everybody seems to apply to you in their difficulties, and I am placed in such a very trying position, that I thought I would apply to you in mine. I had a sleepless, uncomfortable night;" and her eyes filled with tears.

"I think I can save you the telling of part of your story," said Mrs. Althea, gently; "your cousins would sooner have had Mr. Glyn's visits paid to them than to you."

"Just so, dear Mrs. Althea. And they need not have taken it up in that way, because his visits were in fact to my uncle. He came over to play chess with *him;* and then, just because he had happened to be by when the accident occurred, the sight of me put it into his head to ask me how I was, and to say kind and flattering things that the occasion really did not call for; and my cousins thought them quite out of place, and thought *me* out of place too, and said I put myself too forward, and other unpleasant things of the kind. So that, at last, I almost came to the resolution of keeping my room all the mornings; but then, again, I thought, why should I?"

"Why should you, indeed?" said Mrs. Althea.

"Because it would have been very dull, you know, for a constancy; and besides, why should I, because I was unjustly suspected, deprive myself voluntarily of the pleasantest society that came to the house? I felt Mr. Glyn did not like me better than any one else; and, if he *did*, could I help it?" cried Rhoda, with eyes flashing with such injured innocence, that Mrs. Althea could not help laughing.

"Go on, my dear," said she, sympathizing, "you could not."

"So I continued to go on as usual," pursued Rhoda, stoutly, "neither putting myself forward, nor absenting myself from the morning room. I was pretty much sent to Coventry;

but when Mr. Glyn came, he talked nicely to us all, especially to my uncle and me, quite superior conversation, Mrs. Althea, to what I have been accustomed to hear, and when he was gone, I had something to think over that made the time pass pleasantly. However, I could not escape giving offence, do what I would; and, one unlucky day, I was being very severely reprimanded, so that I could not help crying, when Mr. Glyn suddenly came in, and heard and saw something of what was going on, before we were well aware of his presence. From that moment, I think, he adopted a new line of conduct; he paid me attentions that none could overlook; and though I really believe he began to do so for the sake of punishing Anna and Charlotte, which was not a very good motive, you know, still, I could not be quite sure that was all. He seemed to become more earnest, more real; and, as it was impossible not to like him very much, it became a question of anxious interest to me, whether he were trifling with me or not—"

Her voice faltered, and she stopped.

"Well might it become so," said Mrs. Althea feelingly. "I should think him a man of too much honour to carry it so far, if he meant nothing serious."

"Well, it seemed so to me," resumed Rhoda. "I am sure I lay awake many a night, thinking it over. And then, another thing hampered me. If he *were* serious, how was I to act? If I really felt that he could make me very happy, and he felt that I could make him so, was I to repel him simply because my cousins envied me his preference?"

"Certainly not," said Mrs. Althea, with decision. "Even had their feelings been more amiable, there was no call on you for this sacrifice. Your repelling him would not make him like either of them."

"So I thought," said Rhoda; "and I am very glad to have you confirm me in it. But still it depended on an *if.* If he were not serious, I might be doing myself a great injury and making myself very ridiculous by thinking him so. But *others* thought so too; and yesterday evening my uncle, who, good, simple-hearted man, might live in a house full of engaged people without ever finding it out, noticed something that was said to me, and taking it much more in jest than was meant, rallied me on my ' conquest,' and ' only wished it might be one ;' which made matters so much worse, that I had a hearty cry about it in my own room, and thought I could not bear it any longer. I wished mamma were alive, and felt what it was to be an orphan; and then I remembered you, dear Mrs. Althea, and thought

I would come and tell you my griefs like Pamela Bohun, if you would let me."

There was something so confiding and artless in the young girl's manner, that Mrs. Althea was quite touched by it.

"My dear," began she, taking Rhoda's hand, "I know so little of Mr. Glyn—"

"Stay a moment, you have not heard all by any means," said Rhoda, blushing. "This morning, my uncle and cousins were going to ride to Maylands; and Charlotte said something tart about my having the opportunity of a fine *tête-à-tête*. I told her I meant to spend the morning with you, which seemed to please her, and she expressed her approval. I started before they did, that they might see me actually off. I had just reached the bleacher's field, when Mr. Glyn came up with me, walking. You know it was not the road from his house to ours, so that I could not have expected him, nor be accused of waylaying him. He asked me whether I were coming to see you; I said yes; and having said that, you know I could not turn back, nor hinder him from going the same way."

"Why should you?" said Mrs. Althea.

"I don't know," said Rhoda, looking distressed, and faltering; "but he never let the conversation drop for a moment, and at last supported it all himself, for I could not get out a word; and at length he said—oh! I cannot tell you what he said;" and she hid her burning face in her hands.

"There's no need," said Mrs. Althea.

"Just then," said Rhoda, "who should ride past us but Mr. Mildmay! He must have seen us before him ever so long, but I was so pre-occupied, so agitated, I never heard him coming. My face was burning, just as it is now; and looking up, rather startled, to see who was passing us, I met his eye; oh, such a mischievous look! he bowed, and rode on. After that, I could not—"

At this moment, in sailed Mrs. Brand, freshly dressed for dinner, in new ribbons and mitts, not a pin out of place, and with a little bit of fancy-work in her hand. She bowed with great ceremony to Rhoda, looked at her acutely, and seated herself with the air of " Here I shall plant myself."

Rhoda gave Mrs. Althea an expressive glance, rose up and kissed her. " I have been paying an unconscionable visit," said she; " good bye." And Mrs. Althea made no effort to detain her.

Mrs. Brand, with officious civility, insisted on seeing her to the door and opening it for her. Having closed it, she returned to her post, and with a meaning, half contemptuous smile, observed,

"That young lady's secret is easily found out."

"I never try to find out secrets," said Mrs. Althea (who, just then, certainly forgot Pamela); "It does not seem to me very honourable."

"Ah, few people are as good as you," said Mrs. Brand; "Most of us love to hear a secret, and to tell it too. Mr. Mildmay, for example. I found Mr. Knight quite in a rage about it."

"About what?"

"About the report of his intention to leave Collington having spread. He said he had never breathed a syllable of it but to me; I, you know, had only mentioned it to you and to Mr. Mildmay, whom I concluded, from his professional habits, it might be safely entrusted to. Instead of which, Mr. Knight going his rounds this morning, finds every one speaking to him about it; and, on coming home, ever so many tradesmen's bills sent in before Christmas, just as if he were going to run away. The consequence is, he is, naturally, very much offended, and says he must, for his credit's sake, stay over quarter-day, if it be only till the next half-quarter: which inconveniences me, of course, so that I, too, owe Mr. Mildmay a grudge."

"Oh, you must stay here till the half-quarter," said Kitty, who had entered in the midst of the story.

"Rely on it, George Mildmay has spread no reports," said Mrs. Althea. "Why, you yourself heard it from the baker, who, of course, may have told others."

Mrs. Brand, for once, had nothing to reply.

Mrs. Kitty took up a newspaper. "Dear me, there's going to be a grand cattle-show in London," said she. "How I should like to see it!"

"Why should not you run up to town, then?" cried Mrs. Brand. "The change would do you good; and I could take care of Althea."

Mrs. Althea's heart stopped beating; and then went on with a thump.

"That would be a pretty business," said Mrs. Kitty; "No, thank you, not I." Mrs. Althea's heart beat more quietly.

"Dear me," resumed Kitty, in a wondering sort of voice, "what a time it is since I was in London, to be sure! years and years! Gigot sleeves were worn then."

"What frights they were!" said Mrs. Brand. "I always regret having been painted in them. By the bye, it is stupid to have one's own picture. I think I shall give it to you, Kate, for I am sure no one will value it more."

"Oh, thank you!" cried Mrs. Kitty. But where shall I hang it?" looking round.

"There's no room there, Kitty," said Mrs. Althea, following her sister's eye.

"It is just the size of that," said Mrs. Brand, pointing to a three-quarter portrait immediately facing Mrs. Althea.

"Oh, I can't take down my father's picture,

even for yours, Eliza," said Mrs. Kitty. "I will hang it over my bedroom mantel-piece, and then I shall see it continually."

"That wall is damp, and will continue so, as you don't have a fire," said Mrs. Brand: "I observed, to-day, that the paper is peeling off. No; without vanity, I think I may say my picture is too good for an attic, and it will save me a chimney-glass; so I will keep it till you have a more respectable place for it. People will only take it for my younger sister."

"I rather believe," she resumed presently, "I shall be obliged to run home before I close with Mr. Knight, to see about various little matters. Will you go with me, Kate?"

"How can I?" said Mrs. Kitty. "Just consider!"

"Well, I thought Althea might be willing to part with you for a few days, as she is pretty easy now," said Mrs. Brand. "I'm sorry you decline. It would have given you a little change."

Taking Kitty's hand, the next time they were left together, Mrs. Althea wistfully said —

"Dear Kitty, Christmas is near; and all who can, should have a happy Christmas. Why should not you, as Mrs. Brand proposes, run up to town for a few days? Pamela Bohun will soon be home, and would, I am sure, gladly come and take care of me. You could not leave me under better auspices."

"You must be mad, Althea!" cried Mrs. Kitty. "I go to London, indeed! As well go to Jericho, while I'm about it! What have I got to do in London, or what has London to do with me? Stuff and nonsense! You'd wish me back before I had been gone half an hour; and I'm sure I should be wishing myself back too. No, no; London is all very well for those that keep their carriages, and don't care how they pay their bills; but it's no place for me, and I'm not going to budge."

Mrs. Althea felt immensely relieved.

CHAPTER IX.

Merry Christmas.

Now Christmas is come,
Let us beat up the drum,
And call all our neighbours together.
Old Song.

HOW joyous was the approach of Christmas to Pamela! She was going home, and preparing various little gifts for all whom she loved; a pretty knitted shawl for her mother, a warm little rug for her father's feet in the pulpit; smart neck-ties for her sisters, and warm, *bought* gloves for her brothers, who being much accustomed to home-manufactures, set an extraordinary value on anything that came from a shop. Then she had to fabricate ingenious inexpensive prizes for her little pupils after they had gone to bed; often humming some old carol or chant over her work. Then came her turn to receive presents too—Mrs. Glyn gave her, oh! grandeur! a violet and black checked silk dress; Adela and Mab gave her a worked collar and cuffs; and, to crown all, Mr. Glyn, who had been quite animated and pleasant of late, opened the following dialogue on the evening of the first day his mother came down stairs, when they had all dined together in honour of the event, and were sitting sociably round the fire.

"Miss Bohun, monetary transactions are dreadful things; but as your attentions to my little pets are not quite gratuitous, may I, without offence, propose a little settlement between us before we part?"

"Oh! thank you, sir!" said Pamela with undisguised pleasure.

"Here then," said he, smiling; and holding something towards her.

Pamela gratefully received it. "But this is twice too much!" said she hastily.

"Why, you don't suppose I make half-quarters, do you?" said he. "No, no, let us hear no more of it—enough said! Well, mamma, did Forest tell you the news to-day?"

Pamela sat blissfully revolving various extravagances for the morrow. Here were fifteen golden sovereigns: she boldly resolved to spend five. Yes, she would buy a bonnet for her mother, cloth and fringe for mantles for her sisters, pictures and story-books for the young ones, and Southey's Doctor in one double-column volume for her father. All which, being a good bargainer, she achieved. When she showed her purchases to Mrs. Glyn, the old lady was surprised—surprised at the eligible investments, and surprised that Pamela had not laid out a penny on herself. Pamela laughed and looked bright: that was not her way of enjoying the spending of money. Mrs Glyn thought girls of her sort ought to be encouraged: she desired her own maid to assist in cutting out the mantles; so that with her assistance, Pamela's swift little needle sped through its task at over-hours, and accomplished it, just before it was time to pack up for home. She showed her work, with girlish satisfaction, to Mrs. Glyn; and that lady, after much commendation, testified her approval by the donation of an amethyst brooch, that might, perhaps, have cost three guineas and was to all intents and purposes as good as new.

At breakfast-time the next morning Pamela, to her surprise, found that Mr. and Mrs. Glyn and the little girls were going to start for Brighton, immediately after Christmas-day. To Brighton! such an immense distance! All settled after her going to bed, the previous evening? Yes; it seemed one of the privileges of wealth to take no anxious thought about such movements, but to fly about from place to place as freely as a bird flies from spray to spray. The Hills were going too! Then Pamela would lose the pleasure she had promised herself, of some long walks and talks with Rhoda during the holidays. Change of scene was very delightful, doubtless, to those who liked it and felt in want of it: for her part, if so much money were to be spent by her in enjoyment, she would rather have spent it in the summer time than at Christmas, when the days were short, the trees leafless, and influenza lying in wait for victims in every draughty house and damp bed. She would rather spend the genial season among the poor people she knew, and could exchange merry looks and kind words with; rather see her own church decked with ivy and holly than any other; rather sit by her own fire-side than a strange one. Our privileges are equalized a good deal, after all!

And oh! what a happy meeting that was, when she reached home, and was locked in the arms of her fond father and mother, and kissing her sisters and brothers! Every one seemed inclined, at first, to talk at once; and when this tendency was subdued, the interlocutors still spoke very fast, and looked very eager, and laughed very often. Laughter of the heart!

The Squire's Christmas hamper, too, had arrived, running over with good things; and Mrs. Glyn had sent a ham and turkey; and farmer Boates had brought rabbits, and widow Norland had killed them a fat goose; there was no end to the good cheer. Fulk had stories without end to tell of Oxford; but this was no time for them, they must be kept for the evening semi-circle round the fire. Prue and Patty had decked the parlour with holly, and Hugh had taken care to tie a piece of mistletoe to the beam across the ceiling. Pamela's presents were produced, and never were presents so admired, extolled, and valued. She poured her ten bright sovereigns into her mother's lap. Danae's shower of gold was insignificant in comparison! Pamela was happy as happy could be; yet as she flew about the house, it seemed to her so much smaller, colder, and scantily furnished than formerly. But if the draughts, thin and few carpets and scanty curtains kept the house cold, there was enough of family affection in it to make it warm and genial as heart could wish.

"Well," cried Mr. Bohun, sitting down in his warm corner:—

"No glory I covet, no riches I want,
Ambition is nothing to me,"

as long as I have my old helpmate and my dear lads and lasses all about me, doing well and looking well. Mr. Glyn may run away from his home at Christmas time, if he likes it."

"Mr. Glyn is a very nice man, though, papa, in many respects," said Pamela, twining her arm within his.

"Is he so, missy? And in what does his nicety chiefly consist?"

"Niceness, not nicety, papa, please! Nicety is his fault, niceness his merit. He has been very generous, this hard winter to the poor—"

"I know he has, my dear; they bless him for it."

"And he really is very fond of his mother, though he shows it in an odd way. Very fond of his little girls, and kind to them, without spoiling them. Very considerate and polite to me. Kind, in a grand, lordly sort of way, to his servants and dependents in general."

"Why, then, he's all one could wish," said Giles, who was roasting chesnuts.

"No, that's not a sequitur," said Mr. Bohun. "Very good as far as it goes, and perhaps Pamela may in the end make him out what you say, though she has not done so yet."

"Is he a religious man, my dear?" said her mother.

"Well, no—and yet yes," said Pamela, hesitating; "his is not surface religion, you know."

"Much good it would be of, if it were," said Fulk, fillipping a nutshell into the fire.

"I mean, it does not appear much on the surface; but I think, at least I hope it lies underneath."

"Pleasant? no stuff about him?" inquired Hugh tersely.

"Pleasant, *very;* especially lately."

"Why, especially lately?" said her father.

"Well, papa, it may be only my fancy, but I have sometimes thought he must be in love."

"That does not always make men pleasant," said Fulk. "Sometimes they turn desperately egotistical and vapid."

"It has had quite a different effect on Mr. Glyn," said Pamela. "Supposing I am in the right, you know, in my fancy. He has seemed in good humour with everybody.

"What should have made him otherwise before?" asked Hugh.

"He was not cross, only indifferent," said Pamela. "In want of an object, I think."

"And whom is he in love with?" asked Prudence, eagerly.

"Pamela, of course," said Ralph, looking very roguish.

"That's just it, master Witty-pate," said she laughing and pinching his ear. "You have hit it exactly, so I must tell you no more."

"Come, Pamela, tell *me*," said Patience imploringly.

"Ah, I dare say. Why don't you believe Ralph?" said Pamela. "Come, Ralph! I love my love with an A because he is amiable, I hate him because he is avaricious."

"Avaricious and amiable! Oh Pamela!" cried little Charity, clapping her hands.

"I love my love, with an F, because he is funny," burst in Hugh, looking mischievously at Pamela, "I hate him because he is formidable. His name is Forest, and he lives in Fordington. That's what *you* should say!—"

"Hark! here come the carollers," said Pamela; and listening they heard the distant sound of clear young treble voices singing:—

"Peace on earth and mercy mild,
Man with Heaven reconciled."

"How lovely!" murmured Pamela, and the young chatterers became attent and solemnized.

"Which of you can repeat Wordsworth's pretty lines on hearing the waits playing beneath his window?" said Mr. Bohun.

"I can, father," said Fulk, and he did so.

"When the young carollers come here, I must give them some cakes and a cup of warm beer," said Mrs. Bohun.

"That's poetry, mamma," cried Geoffrey laughing.

"It's poetry they'll like very well, Geoffrey. Perhaps their poetry may convert the warm beer into wassail bowl."

"Ah! do let us have a wassail bowl, mother dear!" cried Hugh eagerly. "We did once."

"Once! how grand!" said Mr. Bohun laughing. "These children have almost as vague ideas of wine as Avaro's steeds had of corn."

"Come, mamma, do!"

"Nonsense, you chicks!"

"Charity begins at home, mamma. You ought to centralize your sympathies. If you give those little vagabonds warm beer, you should give your own children wassail bowl."

"It will take a whole bottle of wine," said Mrs. Bohun, hesitatingly.

"I don't believe the real old wassail was made of wine," said Mr. Bohun. "Else, why 'wine and wassail'? it would be tautology."

"Oh, father, don't broach such dreadfully niggardly opinions on Christmas-eve!" cried Fulk. "'Christmas comes but once a year.' There are but thirteen glasses in a bottle: here are your ten children, my mother and you. One glass a-piece, father, and one for manners."

"One glass a-piece, and two for papa," interrupted little Charity.

"Well put in, Caritas, alias Carrots."

"Come, Fulk, you shall get the wine," said his mother, rummaging among her keys,

"Prudence shall boil the spice, and Hugh shall roast the crab-apples."

"'The cook, if he lack not wisdom, shall sweetly lick his fingers,' mamma!"

"You may do as you like about that; meantime, I must go and warm the beer. Cut up the plain cake for them, Patience."

"Papa! please make a rabbit on the wall."

"Willingly. See, Roger, here is a noble rabbit! How he moves his ears! Pretty Bunny!—Ah! I see a strange shadow,—whose profile is that? Somebody coming in. Ha! Mr. Mildmay! This is neighbourly of you!"

"I just dropped in to wish you all a merry Christmas," said George. "You know, I have done so these three years. Have *you* forgotten it?" said he in a lower voice to Pamela, as he took her hand.

"Then that's why we are to have the Squire's turkey for supper," cried Mr. Bohun. "My wife was so sly, she never named you, but I'm sure she thought of you. Come, Mr. Mildmay, it will only be changing the name of your late dinner,—Turkey, sausages, mince-pies, wassail-bowl, at eight o'clock."

"Sir, I shall be most happy."

"'Now, let us sit, though not upon the ground,
And tell strange stories of the deaths of kings.'"

"Your horse, Mr. Mildmay, must be put up."

"Sir, I have seen to his Christmas comforts already, thank you; trusting, not groundlessly, you see, that you would take me in. I wish every poor wayfarer were taken in to as good a fire and as good company this evening, and that's a large wish."

"Where shall you eat your Christmas dinner, Mr. Mildmay?"

"Will you let me eat it *here*, sir?"

"You will help us to make up a baker's

dozen; but remember, thirteen is an unlucky number."

"And there's a coffin leapt out of the fire," cried Hugh.

"Nonsense," said Pamela, "it's a purse."

"As I am not superstitious about coffins or unlucky numbers," said George, "I will make bold to come, with your permission, and in time for church, looking in on Mrs. Althea by the way. Hark! here come the carollers in full force!"

And the full tide of song burst forth in front of the house—

> Hark! the herald-angels sing,
> Glory to the new-born King!

Christmas morning was "frosty but kindly." Mrs. Althea and Mrs. Kitty exchanged fond kisses and good wishes. Their friends had not forgotten them: their larder was full, the post brought kind letters; the parlour was adorned with Christmas greens and Christmas gifts. A reading-desk for Mrs. Althea from Rhoda; a lamp-candle for Mrs. Kitty, from George Mildmay; a pretty tea-urn for both, from Miss Rickards. Many humbler friends had the sisters gladdened in their turn. Trains of thrifty mothers and scantily clad children were seen cheerfully hastening homewards with steaming, savoury messes provided by Mrs. Kitty, or warm additions to their clothing from Mrs. Althea. Mrs. Brand called it "charming! charming!" but was persuaded her dear friends must have spent a great deal of money, and delighted when she heard they had not.

"A merry Christmas to you, my dear Mrs. Kitty!" cried George Mildmay, looking in on his way to church. "I am glad to see you tying up the mistletoe,—of course, I shall avail myself of it."

"George, how can you be so stupid?" said Mrs. Kitty, shaking him off.

"Why, you look as blythe as a bridegroom, George!" said Mrs. Althea, holding out her hand. He took it, and kissed it, saying softly, as he bent over her with a smile, "Perhaps I may be one, some of these days."

Answering her quick look, he added, "I live in hope." Then turning about, "Ladies, I would have you to know it is full time to get ready for church."

"That depends upon how long we take to get ready," said Mrs. Kitty, smartly.

"Well, the bells are going."

"Not all of them, till *we* go," said Mrs. Kitty. "However, Eliza, I believe we have not much time to spare."

"Nor have I," said George, waiting, however, till they had left the room. Then, with eager subdued voice, and mantling colour,

"Mrs. Althea," said he, " I have spoken. She is mine!—we are engaged!"

" How thankful I am! May Heaven's blessing rest on you both! This will indeed make Christmas merry to me!"

" You are always finding your happiness in others! When may she come to you? She is longing for an uninterrupted hour."

" Ah, my dear friend, I seldom have an uninterrupted hour now. However, Kitty and Mrs. Brand are going to see the conjuror to-morrow; they will walk over by daylight, and take tea with a friend in the town first; so that if you and Pamela would not mind a twilight walk—"

" Oh, delightful! Of course, we should mind it very much if it were not for *your* sake, and we shall not have anything to talk about by the way, so you must coddle us and make much of us when we arrive."

"Well, I'll see what I can do. How happy her father and mother must be!"

"Well, ma'am, you forget how short the time has been for telling them yet. But the truth is, I did give dear Mrs. Bohun just one little hint beforehand, which smoothed the way for me wonderfully; and I'll answer for it she has found means, by this time, to tell her husband. Good bye, good bye!"

Mrs. Althea read the Christmas service quietly and thankfully. It was not her first solitary housekeeping on a Christmas morning; and when she thought of the brighter, healthier days, when she had "gone forth with the multitude unto the house of God with the voice of praise and thanksgiving among such as kept holy-day," her heart did not die within her, for she was able to put her trust in Him who was the help of her countenance and her God.

True, the future looked dark; true, years of tedious confinement and increasing infirmity and weakness lay before her, unless a shorter road were unexpectedly afforded to her journey's end. And then poor Kitty would be left alone, unless she cast in her lot with Mrs. Brand.

Well, even that might be for Kitty's comfort. But Mrs. Althea would not look forward; she would confide her future to Him who had already brought her thus far safely on life's journey.

CHAPTER X.

Mrs. Althea's Tea-table.

> We brought our work, and came, you see,
> To take a friendly cup of tea.
> JANE TAYLOR. *Recreation.*

MRS. Kitty and Mrs. Brand had started to see the unparalleled and unrivalled performances of the Wizard of the West, about half an hour; and Mrs. Althea, in her best claret silk dress and French shawl, was lying in sober expectancy of waking bliss in the company of her young friends, when Pamela entered alone, glowing with health and happiness, and threw herself into her arms.

George had some patients round Collington

to see before his day's business was over; but he had walked with her great part of the way, and would be sure to join them before tea; and Pamela was not sorry to have Mrs. Althea to herself for an hour in the first place, as she had so much to say that could not be said in the presence of others. First, there were her schoolroom experiences, which she spoke of in a very cheerful spirit: she did not dislike governessing at all; she had always been fond of children and of teaching, and it was delightful to find herself useful.

> Life is real, life is earnest,
> And this world is not its goal.

And then there was the joy of returning home, which she could never have had if she had not left it: of returning, crowned with home-honours, thanked by her parents as a family benefactress, revered and idolized by her younger brothers and sisters; and with the consciousness of having given satisfaction to her employers. All this would have made up an enviable amount of felicity, even if—

Pamela blushed as she approached the subject of her engagement. It appeared, that there had been of old a kind of boy and girl attachment between George and herself. On his side it had seemed to die out, at any rate had been lost sight of, in the busy scenes of life; while hers had still existed, insofar as to make her feel there was no one she had ever seen whom she liked so much, or who was so calculated to make her happy. But Pamela's upright and earnest nature was not one to expend itself in hopeless longings or vain despairs; she had firmly closed the door against the subject under any guise, as much as in her lay; and it is surprising how our efforts of this kind are seconded, if we make them with a will. Still, the foe, though bound hand and foot, starved out, and asleep, was *alive:* it needed but to loose his bonds, rouse him, and give him food, to make him rise up in renewed vigour. And therefore, when Pamela found that George Mildmay, if he had not loved her all this while, yet had loved her long, loved her now and loved her much, she could return his affection with all the purity and fervour of her heart.

Long before the old and young friend had exhausted all they had to say, George joined them. The fire was bright, the shutters closed, and the curtains drawn; but there was only the cheerful fire-light, though the new and pretty lamp stood in the centre of the table that Mrs. Kitty had generously covered for her sister's guests with numerous varieties of cake and bread, delicate slices of ham and turkey, and glass-saucers of sweetmeats and honey. A gay urn-rug, worked by Miss Rickards, awaited the new urn that had superseded the bright little brass kettle. As soon as George entered, Hannah proudly brought in the urn, loudly hissing and throwing up a prodigious column of steam, and planted it with a mighty and ostentatious effort on the table. Pamela immediately prepared to do the honours; but George begged that the lamp might not be immediately lighted, the fire-light was so pleasant.

He looked beaming with love, good faith, and every honest and manly feeling and affection; notwithstanding which, there was a little frown on his brow, slight as a summer cloud. Both his companions observed it, and he was not one to keep its origin long concealed.

"That Mrs. Brand of yours," he presently began, "what a toad she is!—First, she meets me on the Queen's highway, detains me from my lawful affairs by ever so much gammon, and ends by telling me Mr. Knight is going away;

but begs me to keep it a dead secret. Of course I do; of course she doesn't, but blabs it to one and another, putting each under the same restriction of secrecy, which, of course only makes every one the readier to whisper it. What's the consequence? The tradesmen think Mr. Knight is going to abscond before Christmas, and send in their bills; he, naturally wrathy, complains to Mrs. Brand; she puts it off upon me, confessing that she let it out in my presence, but no other. Let it out, indeed!— I met Knight just now, who looked as black as Le Noir Fainéant; so without any ceremony, I said, 'Mr. Knight, I find there is an uncomfortable impression afloat that I have told people you are going away. I had it from Mrs. Brand; but, I assure you, I mentioned it to no living creature but Mrs. Althea Hall, who was safe to hear it from Mrs. Brand, if not from me.' Would not you have expected this to mollify the fellow? But no, I could see he still owed me a grudge; and though he said a few civil words that meant nothing, he spoilt them by adding, that it might as well have been told the town crier as to you; for that you received and entertained the whole county! This nettled me, I confess; and 'Mr. Knight,' said I, ' if you mean, by entertaining the county, that the lady in question entertains the best of our county families by retailing small local news, I can assure you, you never were more mistaken. No one is less indebted to petty scandals for her power of entertaining her friends, and instructing them, too, than Mrs. Althea:—and so, sir, as I believe I am keeping you from your dinner, I have the pleasure of wishing you good evening!'"

" Well done!" said Pamela, approvingly.

" George," said Mrs. Althea, amused, " you had better leave me to fight my own battles; which will, perhaps, end in my having no battles at all. Mr. Knight may say and think what he likes of me and the county; but it will do me no harm with any one who knows me; and I shall not hear what he says. But nothing would annoy me more than that you should embroil yourself with him, and make him your active enemy, which will hurt you more than him, as he is certainly going away, and may leave a sting behind him."

"A clear stage and no favour, ma'am, is all I desire. Don't let us waste our time by talking or thinking any more on so disagreeable a subject. I thought, to be sure, it would be nice to divide the business with Forest, and take the outlying districts including Collington, which are more fatiguing to Forest than to a light young fellow like me; and Knight's small leavings and his cottage seemed desirable, especially under present circumstances; but we'll find another, won't we, Pamela?"

"Another and a better," said Pamela. "I never was so particularly fond of Mr. Knight's cottage; the walls are so bare, so straight and uninteresting."

"It would be anything but uninteresting to me," said George, "if you were its mistress and I its master."

"Ah, that would make a grand difference, no doubt," said Pamela, laughing. "We can well wait for something better."

"Wait till a house is built? My dearest Pamela!—"

"Well, it will be something to look forward to, and to watch in progress."

"Oh, that will never do."

"I'm afraid it would be too expensive," said Pamela, wistfully. "It must cost a great deal to build a house, even a little one. What a pity we can't build one ourselves!"

"Just put in a brick or two when the humour

suits us, hey? And get the boys to help us for a frolic, on half-holidays. Or this way:— Suppose my laying a wager with somebody— Mr. Glyn, for instance—that I'd build my own house! Then, you know, there would be no shame in doing it. You should carry the trowel and I the hod. Oh, delightful!"

"Ah, something will turn up for us, some of these days—"

"Can't you fancy me, splashing about the lime and water, or doing a neat little bit of masonry?"

"Oh, exactly!"

"If we could even get a house in the shell—"

"With you for the snail? No, that would not do."

"I'm no snail! It's *you* are the snail, all for procrastinating."

"Procrastination is not my nature, is it, Mrs.

Althea? But there is no good in doing things in a hurry; and some things cannot and will not be done in a hurry. Now, for instance, my engagement to Mr. Glyn cannot be given up at the first word—"

"What! not for an engagement to Mr. Mildmay?"

"I've a notion," said Mrs. Althea, "that Mr. Glyn has an engagement of his own in view—if it be not made already—that may make him wonderfully lenient towards you."

"Have you found that out?" said Pamela, smiling, and colouring a little.

"Why, I all but know it. Rhoda had all but told me, when Mrs. Brand came in."

"Ah, that Mrs. Brand!" groaned George. "Pamela! why did you blush when you spoke of Mr. Glyn's engagement?"

"Did I? I don't know—"

"Come; I shall be jealous!"

"I suppose it was because I felt a little ashamed—"

" Of what, pray ? "

" Of being sharp-sighted on the subject. And I may be mistaken yet."

" Oh, I think you are not," said Mrs. Althea. " Rhoda's communications made the matter pretty certain."

" What a nice thing for her! She does not seem very well placed in her present home, and Mr. Glyn can offer her such a nice one! "

" If I had known he had been pre-occupied in that quarter," said George, drawing a deep breath, " it would have saved me some sleepless nights."

" Oh, Mr. Mildmay, how could you be so stupid as to be afraid of him ? "

" *Mr. Mildmay ?* "

" George, then, " softly, and hesitating a little, with a pretty heightening of colour.

"How could I be so stupid?" repeated he absently, and much more occupied in looking at her than in thinking of what he said. "Well, I am sure there was plenty to be afraid of—prosperity, personality, propinquity."

"Dear Mr. Mildmay, the propinquity between the master of the house and the governess is nothing!"

"Ought to be nothing, at any rate," said Mrs. Althea.

"And *can* be nothing, in a well-regulated family like Mr. Glyn's," said Pamela. "We were pleasant and polite to each other; but should never have been anything more, if we had lived to the age of Methuselah."

George burst out laughing.

"Something short of the age of that venerated gentleman," said he, "I should have thought you tolerably safe."

"In the event of this alliance taking place,"

said Pamela, "I dare say they will not want a governess."

"My adorable Pamela, they will not want the children always hanging about them. But they might find plenty of governesses, I should think, at Brighton."

"Brighton is nearly as large as London, I suppose?"

"You dear ignoramus! no!"

"Why should you think governesses so rife there, then?"

"Because it's a place where people are always going and coming, and changing their servants, and changing their governesses."

"Is it a nice place?"

"Very,—for shops and sea, and Mutton's pies, and Silvani's gimcracks."

"Mutton-pies?"

"Mutton's pies. He's the top pastry-cook. I dare say Mr. Glyn is eating one of his pies now."

"Oh no; it is only six o'clock, and Mr. Glyn does not dine till seven. If I were Rhoda, I would alter that."

"If you were Rhoda, you would probably like seven o'clock dinners and Mr. Glyn; instead of one o'clock dinners and George Mildmay."

"You don't dine early, I'm afraid."

"I will, to please you."

"Oh no, I shall not mind it much."

"When a man comes in, throws off his great coat, cloak, or poncho, puts on his shoes, and feels there is nothing between him and midnight, but his dinner, his wife, his wife's tea-table, his book, and his good fire,—it's no bad thing, I fancy!"

"But *you* sometimes have something between—"

"Ah, don't remind me of that horrid surgery-bell! We'll tie it up, my Pamela!"

Chatting thus, on one thing and another, the light-hearted, happy young people needed no entertainment beyond that with which they supplied one another; nor did Mrs. Althea want any beyond hearing them and looking at their blythe faces. The hour came only too soon, when, with all her hospitality, she was obliged to turn them out. Pamela allowed it was quite time to go: they kept early hours at home, and George would have a long dark ride afterwards. George protested against the ride being either long or dark; but he was sure it was time for Mrs. Althea to be in bed and asleep; and, to prevent his needing any other incentives to depart, she did not gainsay it.

"And pray, how are Mrs. Kitty and Mrs. Brand coming home?" said George. "Will they, too, foot it?"

"George, whisper it not in polite circles—

they are coming home in a light, covered cart, with plenty of sacks and matting in it."

"Well, I'm glad to hear it, ma'am, for, with Mrs. Kitty's tendency to the rheumatics, such a long walk on a cold night might be dangerous. Give her some hot negus when she comes back; or, rather, let Hannah make her a treacle-posset, for you must go presently to bed. I, your health's director, insist on it. Good night, dear Mrs. Althea! May you yet have many happy Christmases!"

A tear shone in her eye, but a smile was on her lips, as she shook hands with him, and kissed Pamela.

She could not watch them from the door, but she could listen to their retreating footsteps, and, when those became inaudible, could yet be near them in fancy, and follow them with many a hope, and wish, and prayer. Then she calmly pursued her evening reading; then rang for

Hannah to set the supper-tray for the absentees against their return, and to help her to bed.

The cold, and busy thoughts, kept her awake. At length, she heard them arrive, with much talking and laughing, which became hushed as they entered the house. A man's voice, an unknown voice, seemed among them.

Presently, Kitty, on tiptoe, peeped very guardedly, into her sister's room.

"Is it you, Kitty? Come in! I am not asleep! Have you had a pleasant evening?"

"Very," said Kitty. "It was such fun. Some of the tricks were capital. I'll tell you about them to-morrow. And how do you think we came home?"

"In the spring-cart, to be sure!"

"In Mr. Knight's gig!"

"Oh, Kitty!"

"He was there, and so polite! And Eliza made room for him, so he sat next us all the performance, and made himself quite agreeable. Then, when we came away, he squired us out, and insisted on calling our carriage, and I could not help laughing, because it was a cart; but Eliza felt terribly ashamed, and he, seeing it, and naturally anxious to please his new tenant, offered to drive us home, if we didn't mind the cold, and Eliza said, 'Oh, that will be far pleasanter!' so he did."

"Why, you must have been ready to perish with cold!" cried Mrs. Althea. "Dear me, it was very dangerous!"

"It *was* very cold," said Mrs. Kitty; "but here we are now, and you've left us a famous fire and a good spread. So, now I'll go and give the poor man a tumbler of hot wine and water, and let him go his ways."

"Do you mean Mr. Knight is actually in the house?"

"Certainly. We could not turn him away

from the door, you know," said Kitty. "So I must not leave him any longer, for he is wanting something to warm him, and so am I, for this room is very cold,—good night!"

And Mrs. Althea was left to think her own thoughts upon it.

"If they had been girls of fifteen," thought she, "one need not have been surprised; but Mrs. Brand is always doing something disagreeably surprising; and, oh, Kitty, Kitty, you're not fifteen!"

CHAPTER XI.

The Sisters Sundered.

Our hardest battle may always be our last; though we dare not take it for granted it will be so. Christian only passed once through the Valley of Humiliation; and though he afterwards was scourged by a heavenly chastiser, he took it meekly and went on his way: it did not occur again.

MRS. Althea did not see Mrs. Kitty again for many days. How was this, you will ask? Marry, it requires some little explanation.

On the morning after the wizard's performance, Mrs. Althea, awaking, found herself with a violent cold in her head, and a sore throat. A cold blast of air had blown open her door when Mr. Knight went away, and she had been lying in a draught all night. Mrs. Althea thought the best and simplest remedy for her cold was lying in bed, and told Hannah she should not get up to breakfast.

"I thinks the ladies up-stairs be of the same mind," said Hannah. "I doesn't hear them stirring."

"Perhaps they would like breakfast in bed too," said Mrs. Althea. "If they would, you can make it for us all; I dare say they are tired."

Hannah retreated, shaking her head in an ominous, dissatisfied manner, and muttering that Mrs. Kitty was no ways used to be a slug-a-bed o' mornings. Presently Mrs. Althea heard "the bubbling and loud hissing urn" being carried into the parlour, which was followed by the chink of tea-spoons. She guessed Kitty had come down and was bestirring herself, which was confirmed by some one presently tapping at her bedroom-door. She said,

"Come in!" expecting to see Kitty; when, lo! in came Mrs. Brand.

"May I be admitted?" said she, putting in her head, and leaving the rest of her person in the passage. Then, tip-toeing in, as if Mrs. Althea were asleep,

"Kitty is tired, and, between ourselves, has a little cold," said she, "so I have persuaded her to breakfast in bed. You won't mind it, will you?"

"Dear me, no," said Mrs. Althea. "I thought you had both better do so. Persuade her to remain in bed all day, if she thinks it will do her any good. I should be quite sorry for her to come down on my account."

"That is just what I told her I was sure you would say," said Mrs. Brand; "and her only objection is that you will send up Mr. Forest or Mr. Mildmay to her, if either of them should come."

"If that is all, I promise her I will not," said Mrs. Althea, "so let her keep herself warm with an easy mind. I hope she will be quite well to-morrow."

"Thank you," said Mrs. Brand. "Might I suggest some mutton-broth for dinner?"

"Certainly. It is already ordered," said Mrs. Althea.

"Thank you, thank you," said Mrs. Brand, gliding away, "I am sure Kitty will like it."

"What does the woman mean by her 'thank yous'," thought Mrs. Althea, chafing; does she mean to make out Kitty's comforts less cared for by her sister than her friend?"

About an hour after breakfast, Mrs. Brand stepped in again, in a warm shawl, with her crochet in her hand. Mrs. Althea, preferring to be alone, closed her eyes, as if asleep; for which artifice she was rewarded by seeing through her eyelashes Mrs. Brand tiptoeing about the room, setting it to rights, as she considered, but in reality, putting everything out of its place, and out of Mrs. Althea's reach.

"Please don't move that," said Mrs. Althea, suddenly.

"Oh," said Mrs. Brand, starting, "are you awake? I thought I would come and sit with you a little, that you might not miss Kitty."

"Thank you, you are very kind; but, do you know, I really prefer being alone; for my throat is too sore to make talking very pleasant or safe, and, if left to myself, I shall very likely doze."

"Is there anything I can get for you? Lozenges? liquorice? sage-tea?"

"Thank you, I have, or had, everything within reach. Will you be so good as to replace the bonbonnière by the bed-side?"

"Certainly. Would you like a book?"

"No, thank you."

" Or newspaper?"

"No, thank you. I am never fond of reading in bed; and holding either book or newspaper, would make my arms cold."

" And, by the bye, there is a dreadful draught down this chimney of yours. I should recommend a chimney-board."

"What, when you prevailed on Kitty to sleep up stairs, because she had no chimney in her room?" cried Mrs. Althea.

Mrs. Brand was out of countenance. " And a good thing I did," said she, quickly recovering herself, " for now she is able to have a roaring fire. I recommend you one."

" Oh, no, thank you," said Mrs. Althea, who really felt in want of one, but thought, if she made her bedroom too comfortable, there would be no getting Mrs. Brand out of it.

Shortly afterwards, however, Hannah made

her appearance, with sticks, paper, and coals, and began to lay the fire.

"Is that your idea, Hannah, or Mrs. Brand's?" said Mrs. Althea.

"I doesn't take my orders from Mrs. Brand," said Hannah, indignantly. "I knew you'd want it, and Mr. George would be ordering of it. If Mrs. Kitty lays in bed, I must do the best I can in Mrs. Kitty's place. Mrs. Brand? Bless ye! *she* order you a fire? She orders one for herself, whenever it takes her fancy; but she thinks of nobody else, not she."

"You are mistaken, Hannah; for she offered me a fire just now."

"Offered, indeed! Were she going to pay for it? I should think my missises might order theirselves fires when they wanted 'em, without *her* offers."

Such is poor human nature, that Mrs. Althea could not help feeling a kind of satisfaction in this open partizanship of her maid. She felt it was wrong, and took herself to task for it with sighs and humiliation.

At noon, Mr. Forest called on her. He was afraid she had a touch of the prevailing epidemic, and recommended her keeping in bed till he saw her again. "How's Mrs. Kitty, after her frolic?" said he.

"How came you to know she had had one?" said Mrs. Althea.

"Oh, we doctors have ways and means. My groom was at the conjuror's, and a good many other grooms too, I fancy. The Western Wizard did not draw a very genteel house. Moreover, Mr. Knight sat next to your sister's friend, and Mr. Knight drove your sister and her friend home. There now!"

"Ah, well, it is a disagreeable subject," said Mrs. Althea. "I shall be glad when the man is gone."

"I don't believe he's going," said Mr. Forest.

"What makes you think so?"

"I had better not meddle with other people's affairs, I believe," said she smiling.

Mr. Forest had, to Mrs. Althea's belief, left the house about a quarter of an hour, when she seemed to hear his voice through the walls, from the parlour; and, her senses being quickened by the circumstance, she presently fancied she heard a man's foot stealthily ascending the stairs.

"Mrs. Brand never *can* be candid!" thought she. "After being closeted with Mr. Forest, she is taking him up to see Kitty, who must be more seriously ill than I supposed!"

She hastily rang the bell. Hannah answered it, looking very glum.

"Is Mr. Forest still in the house, Hannah?"

"No, mum."

"I thought I heard him going up to Mrs. Kitty."

"No, mum."

"Are you quite sure?"

"Yes, mum!"—throwing nearly a scuttlefull of coals on the fire.

"I suppose I am a little feverish, and that makes me fanciful," said Mrs. Althea, sinking back on her pillow.

Hannah was evidently in very bad humour, and she therefore would not say anything more to upset her; otherwise, she would presently have asked her whether some one had not been quietly let out of the house door.

"Mrs. Brand is doubtless gone for her walk," thought she. "She lays much stress on regular exercise."

But, soon after, the chance opening of two doors at once, enabled her to hear, for a moment, Mrs. Brand and Kitty chatting very merrily.

"Kitty cannot be seriously ill, to talk and laugh like that," cogitated Mrs. Althea. And this was her only piece of comfort the rest of the day.

The next day passed very much like the first. Mrs. Althea expected to see Mrs. Kitty; but Mrs. Brand appeared instead. "Kate was still in bed. In fact, her cold was rather more troublesome, though nothing at all to signify."

When Mrs. Brand used the expression "in fact," it was generally a sign that the fact was being departed from. Mrs. Althea applied to Hannah.

"Hannah, is Mrs. Kitty very ill?"

"Not as I knows on, mum. Mrs. Brand takes all the waiting on herself."

"Do you mean you've not seen her?"

"Well, ma'am, I've seen her nightcap peeping from under the bedclothes: but she has a cold, she says, and covers herself up close."

"Have you heard her speak?"

"Oh dear, yes, mum."

"Is her voice altered?"

"*Altered*, mum?"

"Like a person's with a sore throat or hoarseness?"

"Oh dear, no, mum, Mrs. Kitty speaks up, like."

As Hannah was still undeniably grumpy, Mrs. Althea gave up the cross-examination in despair, and said,

"Go up stairs, and ask Mrs. Kitty, from me, how she is now."

Hannah went, and returned with, "She says she's purely, thanke'e, mum, and doesn't want for nothing."

"Did you see her?"

"Mrs. Brand told me not to let in the draught, mum."

"Mrs. Brand blows hot and cold about draughts," murmured Mrs. Althea. "If Mr.

Forest or George come to-day, I shall insist on her seeing whichever of them it is."

But neither of them came; and still Mrs. Brand's bulletins were interlarded with "the truth is," and "in fact."

Kitty continued up-stairs, and Hannah grew more and more cross and uncommunicative. Mrs. Althea was in a nervous fever. She was too ill to leave her bed; no one called; and she had nothing to do but to lie still and torment herself with perturbing, improbable conjectures. She was weary, weary! as Mariana in the Moated Grange; almost ready to get one of the ploughmen to carry her up-stairs. As for Mrs. Brand, she quite hated her stealthy tread and rustling gown. When Mrs. Brand. invested *pro tem.* with Kitty's bunch of keys, came to indulge Mrs. Althea with a little chat, it was always to tell her that there was very little wine in the cellar, or the tea was running short, or the pantry window was broken, *Hannah* said by the cat; broken so that a man might put his hand in and help himself to mince-pies without the least difficulty! *She* believed Hannah and some one else played into each other's hands; she thought Hannah was making a purse; she had found one of Mrs. Althea's cotton-reels on the kitchen dresser, hidden away in a tea-cup! Concealment looked like .... well, she would not say what it looked like; but she must own she liked people to be open and above-board.

"*Do* you?" thought the indignant Mrs. Althea.

These visits were terrible inflictions; but Kitty would not be easy unless they were made; and in the intervals, Mrs. Althea could do nothing but listen to the flail in the barn, and the ticking of the clock on the stairs. Could do nothing else? Why, Mrs. Brand said to her daily, "I know you don't mind being alone, because you have such a well-stored mind!" Alas, her mind refused to give up its stores—she could hardly pray, she could hardly think, she could not even lie dozing " in indolent vacuity of thought." Her mind was wide-awake, feverishly so, but it could not meditate, it could only feel. She envied the cat that sat blinking before the fire.

Three days thus passed, without her seeing any one but Mrs. Brand and Hannah; the latter getting so upset that Mrs. Althea began, in dismay, to consider the possibility of her becoming completely unsettled and giving warning. There was terror in the thought. She knew Kitty had words with Hannah now and then, and by no means thought her too excellent to be replaced; but, to Mrs. Althea, who hated strange faces about her, and to whose ways Hannah had become accustomed, the idea of change was distraction. She resolved, if things did not mend in twenty-four hours, to come to an understanding with Hannah the next day.

Things neither mended nor worsened, excepting that Mrs. Althea's illness increased. In the night, she was obliged to ring for Hannah. Hannah was sleeping heavily and did not hear the bell. "Oh, Kitty, Kitty!" thought Mrs. Althea, "it would not have been thus with *you*." She lay still, endured the pain, and did without the remedy.

"What a poor creature am I!" thought she. "How small are my powers of endurance, how much I depend upon others! Mrs. Brand says mockingly what many are in the habit of saying in good faith, and always grieve me by saying— 'I know you have such infinite resources!' Where are they? in what respect have I the advantage of my humblest, most unintellectual neighbour? I can neither frame a prayer with any fervour, nor even recollect an entire hymn. If

I get through a verse, the rest fleets from me, and I find myself tossing and fretting for Kitty."

And thus have thousands felt before you, Mrs. Althea. "What a piece of work is a man! how noble in reason! how infinite in faculties!" And yet what a poor creature he is when laid aside by disease, and weakness, and impaired spirits. Sometimes, indeed, he soars superior to them all; but that is seldom when the pressure is on the nerves; or on the affections.

The best way for a sufferer under trials that *will* make themselves felt, is not so much to grapple with them as foes as to embrace them as friends; saying to each of them in turn, "Come, thou blessed of the Lord! Fit me to inherit the kingdom prepared for me!"

On the fourth day, Mr. Forest called; and he came in, looking almost as cross as Hannah. Mrs Althea's heart began to flutter; was all the world, all her little world, going wrong?

"I have been very poorly since you were here last," said she, deprecatingly, and holding out her hand, "so that it seemed to me as if you were never coming again."

"I suppose," said Mr. Forest bluntly, and taking her hand professionally, not amicably:— "I suppose, Madam, you really *did* think so, by your calling in another medical adviser."

"What can you mean?" exclaimed Mrs. Althea, breathlessly. "What other medical adviser?"

"Who but Mr. Knight, of course?" said Mr. Forest, gruffly.

"My dear Mr. Forest! I have seen no one but you! Never received a professional visit but from you and George Mildmay since the beginning of my illness! How can you have ever imagined it? I can hardly help laughing at the idea!" said she, and the next moment her handkerchief was at her eyes.

"Well," said he, softening a little, "the strangest reports do certainly get about! It is said, in more than one quarter, that Mr. Knight has been seen coming daily out of this house, and that you, for want of confidence in your old advisers, have called him in."

"Never was anything in this world so false! I never even spoke to the man!"

"Well, it seemed strange to me, I must say. After 'all the friendship that we two have shared,'—it was such a breach of professional etiquette, that I felt very angry with the fellow, and certainly rather angry with you. We had gone on so long together, and all the county knew you were, or said you were, so well satisfied."

"So I was: so I am. How *could* the report get about?"

"I heard of it first from John Fox, who said Knight was attending Mrs. Hall. That, of course, meant you. Next I heard it from the Simpsons, who said he was attending one of the Mrs. Halls. That, you know, might do for either of you."

"Either of us? Is it possible that Kitty—"

Mrs. Althea rang the bell with energy.

"Hannah!" said she with severity, as soon as her domestic appeared, "how dared you keep from me that Mrs. Kitty was so ill?"

"Law, mum," burst forth Hannah, with an air of being greatly injured, "'twern't no secret of mine, but Mrs. Brand said it was to be kept one, and Mrs. Kitty said so too."

"How dared you conceal from me," pursued Mrs. Althea with increasing heat, "that Mr. Knight was attending Mrs. Kitty?"

"There! I wipe my hands of the whole kit on'em," said Hannah, suiting the action to the word by wiping her hands in her apron; "'T were no affair of mine—I knowed ye wouldn't like it; but, were I to tell if they said I wasn't to?"

"How often has he been, Hannah?"

"Three times, mum."

"What does he say is the matter with her?"

"Well, mum, I made bold to ask, and they told me Harry's shoes."

"Harry's shoes!" ejaculated Mrs. Althea.

"Harry's slippers, then," said Hannah, getting bewildered and impatient.

"Erysipelas," interposed Mr. Forest.

"That's the word, sir," said Hannah.

"Nothing more likely," said Mr. Forest, "to induce an attack of erysipelas in the head than the cold night-drive in Mr. Knight's gig."

"Hannah," said Mrs. Althea, who was in tears, "go up directly to Mrs. Kitty, and say, Mr. Forest is coming to see her."

"No, no, not I," interrupted Mr. Forest; "*I* don't interfere with other men's practice."

"But, if you don't see her, I shall never

know the real truth about her state—it will never be told me till too late....Perhaps I may even never see her again." And Mrs. Althea wept bitterly.

"Psha!" cried Mr. Forest, "I never can stand a woman's tears; least of all yours. So step up, Hannah, and say, I'm coming just to pay a friendly visit. I must follow pretty close, or Mrs. Brand will be down upon me."

Mrs. Althea continued shedding tears during his absence, which was very short. "I wash my hands of it," said he, shrugging his shoulders. "Knight has begun, and Knight may make an end. The fellow can't well blunder in so simple a case, and will probably bring her through safe enough."

"*Is* it erysipelas?"

"Oh yes, it has passed right over her head and is coming down now over her forehead, like a red curtain—"

"Poor Kitty! Oh, don't forsake her."

"Nay, 'tis she has forsaken me—she won't have a word to say to me—when I got upstairs, she called out, 'Oh, my goodness, Mr. Forest, don't come in—I hav'n't got on my best night-cap!' And then there was such tittering and giggling, as might have suited a couple of school-girls, rather than middle-aged ladies. As if I cared about her night-cap!— I'll come and see *you*, Mrs. Althea, since the report about your calling in Knight is false; but as for Mrs. Kitty,—as she has brewed, so she must bake. George Mildmay generally takes the Collington round; George Mildmay has lately had it pretty much to himself— George Mildmay may make friends or foes with Mr. Knight as he pleases—I am going to do neither one nor the other."

It struck Mrs. Althea that an ill-concealed tone of peevishness—when speaking of George

Mildmay—might have something to do with the successful wooing of Pamela.

"But, Mr. Forest," said she, anxiously, "Erysipelas is a very dangerous thing, sometimes, is it not? Do you think Kitty will take it heavily?"

"Can't say, indeed—very likely; for she is an inflammatory subject."

"Dear me; it must be very painful in the head, I should think?"

"Rely upon it, it is."

"Do you think she will get light-headed, towards night?"

"Very likely."

"And with nobody to nurse her but Mrs. Brand! Oh, my case *is* hard!" And the tears again trickled down her pale cheeks.

"My dear Mrs. Althea," said Mr. Forest, kindly, "let us make the best of things. It may be a lucky thing for us all that Mrs. Brand is here. You and I don't like her, but Mrs. Kitty does; and she will have a nurse to her mind, and one who, for her own credit's sake, will show herself both able and willing."

" I hope she may," said Mrs. Althea, drying her eyes. " I am sure Kitty is welcome to the whole of her services. Hannah is quite enough for me; and when I cannot have her, I would rather be left quite alone."

" Ah, you know well how to bear solitude—your mind affords inexhaustible resources;" said Mr. Forest, patronizingly repeating the old hackneyed axiom, as if there were really something new in it. He went away, pleasing himself that this judiciously-administered compliment had made Mrs. Althea quite comfortable; while she, after a fleeting smile at its being so wide of the mark, fell thinking again upon Kitty.

" Oh, my case *is* hard!" She had never

uttered that sad lament during the long season of her captivity; but she felt it to be very, very hard, now that it prevented her nursing her dear and only sister.

Mrs. Brand came in with one of her made up smiles and melo-dramatic attitudes. "Well," cried she, stifling a little affected laugh, "it was well our two medical men did not meet on the stairs—Knight had but just gone."

"I *cannot* laugh," said Mrs. Althea, sternly. "You have done me the greatest harm in your power—put my sister into the way of getting dangerously ill—and put it out of my power to see her."

Mrs. Brand stood with an air of mock surprise. "My dear Althea," cried she, "what *are* you thinking of?"

"I have said my say," said Mrs. Althea, doggedly.

"My dear creature, you hardly know what

you *have* said. I am sure you did not mean to wound me. I am sure nothing could be farther from your intention than being rude to me; han saying the most cutting things that ever were said to me in my life! *I*? put dear Kate in the way of being ill? Why, was it not a medical man who proposed the thing? Might not I have been the victim myself? Was I a likely person to endanger the health of my dearest friend? a friend who never said a cutting thing to me? Why, am I not now proving my attachment to her by nursing her in what is considered by some an infectious complaint?"

"I am really too ill to have any altercation about it," said Mr. Althea, turning her face to the pillow. "You say you love her, and I conclude you do. I hope, therefore, that she is in safe and kind hands. Do your best for her, and that will be the truest kindness to us both."

"I can assure you, I don't need prompting to a duty that will be such a pleasure," said Mrs. Brand, looking at her watch. "Dear me, I must return to the dear invalid. It is a quarter past four, I declare."

Just then, the old clock on the stairs struck four.

"Hannah!" said Mrs. Althea authoritatively to her servant, who entered as Mrs. Brand passed out, "set that clock forward! Nothing in this house over which I have any power, shall tell lies if I can help it."

"Then you'd better alter Mrs. Brand's watch, mum," said Hannah, "instead of the clock."

CHAPTER XII.

The Sisters Re-united.

It would have been more honourable of David to ask for the strength of an ox to bear his trials, than for the wings of a dove to flee from them.—MATTHEW HENRY.

THE two sisters were very ill. Mrs. Kitty's fever ran high, she was delirious; and Mr. Knight and Mrs. Brand had rather a troubled sense of their responsibility. Mrs. Brand, dismayed at Kitty's swollen and fearful appearance as the eruption crept down her face, and constantly employed in dipping soft rags in lotion and applying them to the skin, took Mrs. Althea at her word, and gave her very little of her company; so little that Mrs. Althea, in Hannah's necessary absences about her ordinary work, was literally neglected, and often in want of aid which she would have been thankful to receive even from Mrs. Brand. She had desired Hannah to get a girl to wash up and be generally useful; but the girl was ignorant and uncouth, broke or cracked nearly as much as she washed, and required so much supervision as to give Hannah very little more time. Then a char-woman was summoned, who had a great gift for eating, drinking, gossiping, and sitting long over her meals. She seemed a worse help than the girl. Hannah's face grew more and more sour; Mrs. Althea's spirits became lower and lower; and when George Mildmay came in one day and found the front door ajar, the cold north wind blowing in on Mrs. Althea, who was helplessly coughing, crying, and ringing for the women shut up in the kitchen, he quite stormed—made his own way, first into the kitchen, then up to Mrs. Brand, whom he met on the landing-place, and rebuked in no measured terms for the condition in which he had found Mrs. Althea; assuring her, with a menacing brow, that before the day was out, he should provide her with some one who would not neglect her.

Mrs. Brand turned white and then red, as alarm and hate reigned alternately; but without minding her changes of colour, George boldly stalked in to the bedside of Mrs. Kitty, who was lying in a sort of stupor, with her eyelids too swollen to unclose. There was not much comfort to carry to Mrs. Althea from that quarter; he was guilty of a pious fraud when he went down and told her that Mrs. Kitty had taken the complaint heavily, but would do well. Hannah, repentant and alert, had been repairing her neglects in his absence, and Mrs. Althea, with everything comfortably arranged about her, was now lying still, though with tear-stained cheeks, incessant cough, and a pulse so weak and irregular, that George's heart sank as he felt it. He supplied her with liquid as tenderly as a woman: talked to her soothingly and hopefully; reminded her of heavenly consolations; and promised her that Pamela should be with her as soon as he could drive her over, to be with her till she was in the parlour again. Oh, what balm to a sore heart there was in every look, word, and accent. And did *he* feel no repayment in his own bosom? There was a tear in his eye as he stooped over her and wished her good-bye; a genuine "God-be-with-you:" and other tears started into his eyes as he drove off.

The expectation of happiness is all but happiness itself. Mrs. Althea was dangerously and painfully ill, but she lay as still and composed as her cough would let her. In a couple of hours Pamela was at her side; those sweet eyes, full of love, met hers whenever she raised her heavy eyelids; those gentle hands ministered to every want; those light feet trod noiselessly the floor. Everything, as if by magic, went right; the kettle on the hob did not boil over, slates in the fire did not explode and scatter about the room; hinges of doors did not creak; windows no longer rattled for want of having the catches fastened; the barley-water did not chill; the chimney did not smoke. Often, often did those well-worn, but never to be hackneyed lines, recur to the grateful Mrs. Althea:—

> When pain and sickness wring the brow,
> A ministering angel thou!

Need it be said, that under the incessant care of George and Pamela, Mrs. Althea became better? For a few days and nights, she was on the brink of the grave; but gradually the alarming symptoms abated, and she slowly but surely improved. Then, at intervals, came sweet and restoring snatches of converse with her loved companion, who proved mighty in the Scriptures, and full of original and high-souled thought. George would linger by the half-hour together, to hear these two talk of one thing and another; Mrs. Althea saying little, but drawing out Pamela's stores of mind so nicely; and Pamela appearing in the most advantageous light, in the performance of the kindest offices, and in the revelation of higher and deeper thoughts and feelings than would otherwise have been called forth. He had always considered her the most charming girl in the world, but now,—

> He saw her upon nearer view,
> An angel; yet a woman too.

When Mrs. Brand, who was getting dreadfully weary of Mrs. Kitty's bed-room, except during Mr. Knight's visits, stole in on pretence of being anxious to know how dear Mrs. Althea was getting on, she found herself *de trop*. But she had her seasons of refreshment; the friends of Mrs. Althea and Mrs. Kitty, learning from George and Mrs. Forest how ill they were, called continually to inquire, and sent in everything at hazard that they thought likely to be fancied by the invalids; consequently, Mrs. Brand, ruling the larder, fared luxuriously: and instead of confining herself so rigidly to Mrs. Kitty's apartment, she proceeded to entertain visitors, in gloves and her best caps, enlarging on Kitty's late danger and present disfigurement, and not sparing those praises of self which are said to be no recommendation. Pamela, finding her continually thus occupied, availed herself of the opportunity to look in on Mrs. Kitty, who, very unsightly in her appearance, and very weak after the fever had left her, was in low spirits, and much given to wonder why Eliza was so long away. She was also fidgety about Mrs. Althea, though by no means aware of what her late danger had been, till Pamela spoke of it. Then Mrs. Kitty became very much agitated; she had been kept in the dark, she had been wanted; she must and would see dear Althea.

Mrs. Kitty was no longer in bed; she was sitting up by the fire, in a large easy chair, stuffed full of pillows, attired in various garments of loose flannel, with a sort of horseman's coat over all. She would go down, that she would, if it were only to give one kiss to her dear Althea.

Pamela was afraid of the consequences, and tried to dissuade, but in vain. Hearing Hannah on the stairs, she called her in to the rescue, but without success. She had no mind to summon he only effectual person, Mrs. Brand, who was surrounded by a circle of morning callers in the parlour. The opportunity was propitious, Pamela felt that in Mrs. Kitty's case, she should have availed herself of it: and Hannah, after a moment's pause, set down the caudle-cup of arrow-root in her hand, before the fire ; and then, saying, " You carried Missis once, so there's no reason why I should not carry you," —suddenly enveloped her from head to foot in a blanket, snatched her up in her sturdy arms, and triumphantly bore her down stairs.

Mrs. Althea, unprepared for such a visitation, though Pamela had made a vain effort to get the start of Hannah, who took up the whole breadth of the stairs, was utterly confounded when she saw Hannah bear in this struggling mass of blankets and flannels, which when Mrs. Kitty had fought a way for her head out of it, disclosed her poor, altered face. The meeting was too much for the sisters—they stretched out their arms to one another before they could be brought together; locked each other in a strict embrace, and burst into tears. Pamela, kneeling up on the bed to support Mrs. Althea, wept too, and Hannah indulged in a quiet roar under her apron.

Fancy George Mildmay entering in the midst of this tableau! To close the scene, fancy Mrs. Brand standing in the doorway!

There is not much more we shall tell. Some things, however, require to be told of. How that Mrs. Brand fell into a rage, at the use Kitty had made of her absence; how George (out of Mrs. Althea's hearing) had made the ironical remark, "When the cat's away, the mice will play." How that Mrs. Brand recriminated by saying that he wanted to injure Mr. Knight by spoiling his case; how George resented this, as a speech unbecoming a lady, and wished to know in what way he had inter-

Bever Hollow. 241

fered with Mr. Knight throughout Mrs. Kitty's illness. How Kitty was quite sure Eliza had meant all for the best, but must own she felt deeply hurt that Althea's danger had been concealed from her; how Mrs. Brand must own she thought this was rather an unexpected return for her unwearied watchfulness, and could not have supposed Kate could be so ungrateful.

However, it was plain, Kate was *now* under foreign and malign influence; Kate, forgetful of the recent past, would never see things in their true light any more; she, Mrs. Brand, was evidently no longer wanted—a newer face was preferred; Miss Bohun could make herself very agreeable down stairs, and up-stairs too, and would doubtless find it agreeable to herself to remain there as long as Mr. Mildmay was calling every day and paying absolute visitations, to the neglect of his other patients. She,

Mrs. Brand, must succumb before the rising sun; there was a good old saying, though a vulgar one, that too many cooks spoiled the broth; *she* had made Kate's broth many a day, without one speck of fat on it; she hoped her new cook, metaphorically to call her so, would do as well.

Mrs. Brand expected Kate to be subdued by this tirade; but, on the contrary, Kate resented it. Eliza was saying a great many things that were untrue and exaggerated, which she would be sorry for when she cooled. Mrs. Brand was never cooler, and had said nothing she should ever be sorry for, because she had said nothing that was either untrue or exaggerated.

When contending parties reach the logical point of contradictory opposition, Peace unfurls her wings in despair, and soars back to her own blue heaven.

And ruder words will soon rush in,
To spread the breach that words begin;
And eyes forget the gentle ray
They wore in friendship's smiling day,
And voices lose the tone that shed
A tenderness round all they said—
Till, fast declining, one by one,
The sweetnesses of love are gone.

Thus was it with Mrs. Brand and Mrs. Kitty. The former, thinking her services too valuable to be yet spared, took a high tone, and said that she was clearly no longer wanted nor wished for, and should therefore go elsewhere, to friends more desirous of her company, —" She had had a letter." Kate was sorry she should think her nursing undervalued; she felt truly grateful for it, but it was not a propitious time to say so now, as she saw Eliza would not believe her. She hoped Eliza would be happy wherever she was going, and see things in a truer, kinder light when they were apart. Mrs. Brand swallowed a hasty answer, snatched up her work-bag, and went off to answer her letter and pack up.

She was really going; but a few days necessarily intervened. In the first place, she had nowhere immediately to go to, till her way was paved a little. In the second, she must see Mr. Knight, and get rid, somehow, of their half-settled arrangement, which, on her part, had never been really in earnest. Lastly, she had made much profession to morning callers of her devotion to the sisters, and it would have an ill appearance if she forsook them too abruptly, as she was not leaving any one behind her to tell her story as she would like it told.

She kept staying on, therefore, on sufferance, as it were, to arrange her own plans and suit her own convenience. Perhaps she was in secret hope that Kitty would give in; but Kitty, when her temper once was up, took long to recover herself. She bore herself so bluntly to the late friend of her bosom, that Mrs. Althea, hearing Pamela's report of the state of parties, compassionated Mrs. Brand, and was very near being so soft as to ask her to remain a little longer as a personal favour.

From this weakness, George and Pamela saved her. Meanwhile, Miss Roberta Rickards, who had been one of the morning visitors, and who had felt indignant at the way in which Mrs. Brand had assumed the airs of lady of the house, and denied her access to Mrs. Althea, now, under the milder nature of Pamela, obtained the admittance she had before sought in vain. Greatly shocked at Mrs. Althea's appearance, and still resenting Mrs. Brand's veto, Miss Rickards begged Pamela to take a little of the relaxation she surely had well earned, while she spent a half hour with her old friend. Pamela withdrew, and Miss Rickards began to unfold to her invalid listener the various delinquencies of Mrs. Brand; not only by giving herself airs that were quite unbecoming a person of so little consequence, but mischievously colouring and twisting even the simplest domestic incidents to every chance visitor, so that any uninformed person might have supposed that the sisters led a cat and dog life; that Mrs. Althea's whims were insupportable, and that she was now being made a tool of by Pamela and George Mildmay, who were suiting their own purposes of constantly seeing one another by their sedulous attendance on her.

When Mrs. Althea heard this, she was far too indignant to feel any disposition, even from compassion, to induce Mrs. Brand to prolong her stay. Kitty was now sufficiently convalescent to be established, much wrapped up, by the parlour fire; and as Mrs. Brand's kind ministrations were much remitted or ostentatiously paraded, Pamela found it desirable to attend to both her friends, which Mrs. Althea's daily amendment enabled her to do without defrauding her of her prior claims. Mrs. Althea, indeed, considered herself able to return to her sofa; but George, with a knowing look and smile, advised her to continue in her room till Mrs. Brand was fairly out of the house.

That hour arrived. George himself handed her into the old yellow fly that was to convey her to the next town. On returning to the house, he found Mrs. Kitty shedding a few tears. "Come," said he, kindly, and sitting down by her as he spoke, "Know your true friends from your false ones. That lady who has just left you is no real friend to any one but herself. She is fond of power, and fond of mischief-making. Remember what Solomon says, 'A whisperer divides friends.' If she had been here much longer, she would have alienated you from Mrs. Althea."

"Oh, no, no! No human power could do that!"

"Well, she would have done her best in that way, at any rate. She had not even a humane concern in your sister."

And he forcibly depicted the condition in which he had found Mrs. Althea, deserted by all, and in want of assistance. Kitty was greatly moved. "No true friend to me," said she, "no woman of any feeling, could have so neglected my sister."

"Enough said: we won't think any more of her," said George. "Now we will carry in Mrs. Althea, and set her face to face with you, and stir the fire, and have a jolly tea, and Pamela shall make the tea, and I'll be as happy—we'll *all* be as happy as kings; and a good deal happier!"

And so they were; and George would not let Pamela leave his and her old friends, nor would Mr. and Mrs. Bohun receive her home till Mrs. Kitty was quite brisk and blooming again, and Mrs. Althea was as well as she was ever likely to be in this world, and quite comfortable and happy. George contrived to see them every day; generally in the evening, when his work was over, and he could enjoy a long, uninterrupted fire-side chat. During these blissful evenings, it would be difficult to say which of the four was happiest.

"Surely," says John Foster, "the great principle of continued interest, in those who love one another, cannot be to talk always in the style of simple, direct personality; but to introduce personality into the subject; to talk of topics, so as to involve each other's feelings, without perpetually talking *at* each other."

One evening, George told them with glee, that he had been offered a capital opening, as far as money went, in Tasmania; but that, having no fancy for expatriation, he had gone straight to Mr. Knight, and rubbed out old scores, by handsomely offering him what he had no mind for himself. "And, do you know, the fellow was quite touched, and said it would be the making of him, with so much about my generosity and so forth, that I was ashamed. I told him I should pick up some amends in Collington, and he said he would leave me the good will, and the cottage too, if I liked it; and I told him I certainly should. I laughed, and told him he had better take out a wife. He must sail in a fortnight."

And in a fortnight he sailed; and took out a wife. Mrs. Althea and Mrs. Kitty received wedding cards.—From Mr. and Mrs. Charles Glyn? Oh, that was soon afterwards. From Mr. and Mrs. Mildmay? *They* sent *cake*. From Mr. and Mrs. Knight! Mr. Knight had married Mrs. Brand!

THE END.

R. CLAY, PRINTER, BREAD STREET HILL.

Trieste

Trieste Publishing has a massive catalogue of classic book titles. Our aim is to provide readers with the highest quality reproductions of fiction and non-fiction literature that has stood the test of time. The many thousands of books in our collection have been sourced from libraries and private collections around the world.

The titles that Trieste Publishing has chosen to be part of the collection have been scanned to simulate the original. Our readers see the books the same way that their first readers did decades or a hundred or more years ago. Books from that period are often spoiled by imperfections that did not exist in the original. Imperfections could be in the form of blurred text, photographs, or missing pages. It is highly unlikely that this would occur with one of our books. Our extensive quality control ensures that the readers of Trieste Publishing's books will be delighted with their purchase. Our staff has thoroughly reviewed every page of all the books in the collection, repairing, or if necessary, rejecting titles that are not of the highest quality. This process ensures that the reader of one of Trieste Publishing's titles receives a volume that faithfully reproduces the original, and to the maximum degree possible, gives them the experience of owning the original work.

We pride ourselves on not only creating a pathway to an extensive reservoir of books of the finest quality, but also providing value to every one of our readers. Generally, Trieste books are purchased singly - on demand, however they may also be purchased in bulk. Readers interested in bulk purchases are invited to contact us directly to enquire about our tailored bulk rates. Email: customerservice@triestepublishing.com

You May Also Like

Longmans' English Classics; Dryden's Palamon and Arcite

William Tenney Brewster

ISBN: 9780649565733
Paperback: 170 pages
Dimensions: 6.14 x 0.36 x 9.21 inches
Language: eng

Hour by Hour; Or, The Christian's Daily Life

E. A. L.

ISBN: 9780649607242
Paperback: 172 pages
Dimensions: 6.14 x 0.37 x 9.21 inches
Language: eng

www.triestepublishing.com

You May Also Like

Joseph Guy's School Expositor; Or, the Learner's New Spelling Assistant

Joseph Guy, Jun.

ISBN: 9780649619146
Paperback: 140 pages
Dimensions: 6.14 x 0.30 x 9.21 inches
Language: eng

The Lost Found, and the Wanderer Welcomed

W. M. Taylor

ISBN: 9780649639663
Paperback: 188 pages
Dimensions: 6.14 x 0.40 x 9.21 inches
Language: eng

www.triestepublishing.com

You May Also Like

Report of the Department of Farms and Markets, pp. 5-71

Various

ISBN: 9780649333158
Paperback: 84 pages
Dimensions: 6.14 x 0.17 x 9.21 inches
Language: eng

Catalogue of the Episcopal Theological School in Cambridge Massachusetts, 1891-1892

Various

ISBN: 9780649324132
Paperback: 78 pages
Dimensions: 6.14 x 0.16 x 9.21 inches
Language: eng

www.triestepublishing.com

You May Also Like

Three Hundred Tested Recipes

Various

ISBN: 9780649352142
Paperback: 88 pages
Dimensions: 6.14 x 0.18 x 9.21 inches
Language: eng

A Basket of Fragments

Anonymous

ISBN: 9780649419418
Paperback: 108 pages
Dimensions: 6.14 x 0.22 x 9.21 inches
Language: eng

Find more of our titles on our website. We have a selection of thousands of titles that will interest you. Please visit

www.triestepublishing.com

Lightning Source UK Ltd
Milton Keynes UK
UKOW01f1536231017
311488UK00016B/3476/P